"With *Out of the Fire*, Jennifer Shepard Payne pro
cally and spiritually based, and much-needed ap
standing and addressing the mental health issues experienced by Black
Americans daily. Each chapter provides clarity in understanding through
culturally responsive empathy. This research-based text rebukes old par-
adigms, shares practical and clever points of reflection, while offering
nuanced strategies toward healing."

> —**Cheryl Fields-Smith, PhD**, professor of elementary education
> at the University of Georgia

"It is the rare scholar and practitioner that integrates research, empathy,
warmth, and care together to help communities transform and heal.
Jennifer Shepard Payne's *Out of the Fire* exemplifies such characteristics.
Every therapist, counselor, and counselee should read and learn from
Shepard Payne's skillful guidance in this book to help support healing in
the Black community and diaspora. This is a much-needed work."

> —**Regina Chow Trammel, PhD, LCSW**, professor of social
> work at Azusa Pacific University, psychotherapist, and author
> of *A Counselor's Guide to Christian Mindfulness*

"In *Out of the Fire*, Jennifer Shepard Payne provides practical and
thoughtfully described tools for developing the skills to thrive after we
deal with the trauma of structural and systemic racism. *Out of the Fire*
includes a wealth of stories and examples that helps humanize the challenges we face. Despite being a book about dealing with trauma, *Out of
the Fire* provides asset-based and positive tools to promote healing and
well-being."

> —**Derek M. Griffith, PhD,** founder and codirector of the
> Racial Justice Institute, and professor of health management
> and policy at Georgetown University

"Jennifer Shepard Payne provided a rich and detailed explanation of racialized trauma and the strategy for mitigating the effects through acceptance and commitment therapy (ACT). This book makes the case for why ACT is a therapy that would appeal to the Black community. Through analogies and stories grounded in research, *Out of the Fire* will be a game changer for those that care about mental health and well-being, especially in the Black community."

—**Tahira Reid Smith, PhD**, cofounder of Black in Engineering

"In *Out of the Fire*, Jennifer Shepard Payne provides a culturally informed, evidence-based, and highly practical guide to thriving that will be life-changing for generations of African Americans and the mental health professionals who support their healing. She has brilliantly tailored ACT to speak the language and reflect the lived experiences of the African American community!"

—**Robyn L. Gobin, PhD**, licensed psychologist, associate
    professor at University of Illinois at Urbana Champaign,
    and coauthor of *The Black Woman's Guide to Overcoming*
    Domestic Violence

"All suffering is not created equal. A powerful and much-needed resource that speaks directly to the unique experiences of Black Americans. Sharing a combination of compelling personal stories, case vignettes, and experiential practices, Jennifer Shepard Payne guides readers to develop the skills necessary to rise from the ashes of systemic oppression, intergenerational trauma, and pain. *Out of the Fire* is THE guide for learning to thrive with meaning and purpose."

—**Jill Stoddard, PhD**, author of *Be Mighty*, and coauthor
    of *The Big Book of ACT Metaphors*

OUT
OF THE
FIRE

Healing Black Trauma

Caused by Systemic Racism Using

Acceptance and Commitment Therapy

JENNIFER SHEPARD PAYNE, PHD, LCSW

New Harbinger Publications, Inc.

Publisher's Note

This publication is designed to provide accurate and authoritative information in regard to the subject matter covered. It is sold with the understanding that the publisher is not engaged in rendering psychological, financial, legal, or other professional services. If expert assistance or counseling is needed, the services of a competent professional should be sought.

Copyright © 2022 by Jennifer Shepard Payne
New Harbinger Publications, Inc.
5674 Shattuck Avenue
Oakland, CA 94609
www.newharbinger.com

Cover design by Amy Daniel; Acquired by Georgia Kolias; Edited by Diedre Hammons

---

Library of Congress Cataloging-in-Publication Data

Names: Payne, Jennifer Shepard, author.
Title: Out of the fire : healing black trauma caused by systemic racism using acceptance and commitment therapy / Jennifer Shepard Payne, PhD, LCSW.
Description: Oakland, CA : New Harbinger Publications, [2022] | Includes bibliographical references.
Identifiers: LCCN 2022029861 | ISBN 9781684039883 (trade paperback)
Subjects: LCSH: Acceptance and commitment therapy. | Racism--Psychological aspects. | African Americans--Psychology. | Post-traumatic stress disorder--Treatment. | BISAC: SELF-HELP / Post-Traumatic Stress Disorder (PTSD) | PSYCHOLOGY / Movements / Cognitive Behavioral Therapy (CBT)
Classification: LCC RC489.A32 P39 2022 | DDC 616.85/21008996073--dc23/eng/20220816
LC record available at https://lccn.loc.gov/2022029861

Printed in the United States of America

24   23   22

10   9   8   7   6   5   4   3   2   1   First Printing

To my God, the wind beneath my wings.

To my entire village, past and present, who shaped, taught, supported, and collaborated with me. You know who you are.

Through you, I rise like a phoenix out of flames
to help pull others out of the fire.

Contents

Preface

I'm sick of shifting. I'm sick of dancing to-and-fro, slithering
  between Afro and "mainstream" mentalities,

Sliding on the attire of appropriateness.

At home in my robe of Blackness in Black spaces and wearing
  the cloak of conventionalism in white spaces.

The camouflage is too tight for me. It chokes me at the
  neckline.

I. Can't. Breathe.

But I've assimilated, though! I've standardized myself,
  conformed myself. I've whittled myself down to become
  non-threatening in non-Black spaces! I have attained!
  I have arrived!

But what have I attained?

I have attained doctorates and education upon education.
  Yet I am Still. Not. Accepted.

By reason of the color of my skin, I too can die daily.

Through circumstantial combination of place and police
  officer

Gawking, staring, glaring me down, positioning me on the
  curb, down low

Lower to the ground than the posture of prayer

Making me bow and kneel…and then kneeling on me

Knee on my essence, suppressing, squeezing

Until I remember the love of my mom's embrace long gone

Until my breath stops.

I have been on that curb. I have been interrogated, humiliated, embarrassed.

I have been pulled to that curb by police officers, unsettled and restless

I have been humiliated by cops. "Did you hide it in your coochie?"

As if he desired to dig in sacred spaces, to reach and grab from my essence.

Always abiding by society's edicts, structures, standards.

Yet coochie-threatened on a curb on a dark secluded street.

I have been brought down low to the curb at school, teased by white peers

While studying doctoral things, lofty ideas, high notions, astute ideas

Asked in a mixed company, "Do you know Homey the Clown?"

While presenting at a conference with white colleagues,

Peach-faced hotel patron asks me, "Take my bags to my car."

In the midst of proper introductions, I am "Dr.," earned from UCLA

Having my hair touched without permission by white, wrinkled hands.

While teaching with purpose, heart, focus, fervor, frivolous faculty evals downgrade me to "knowing nothing" by biased beings.

I have been on that curb. I keep being brought back to that curb. Despite the shifting.

I'm sick of shifting.

—June 1, 2020

We Are Continuously Burned by Fire

Fire does not make fire, only ashes.

—African proverb, author unknown

I can recall the fiery inferno that burned in me the day that George Floyd died as if it were yesterday. May 25, 2020, on a Monday. I am a university professor, and I was using that Monday to do teaching preparation. I sat at my desk in my home office, something that all of us professors had been doing since March because of COVID-19. The viral video of George Floyd's murder was circulating at that time.

I don't always click on videos. Lord knows that there have been many other videos before this one. But I clicked. And my life immediately changed.

There had been so many police incidents before this one, but this one stood out, even more than Rodney King's verdict. Rodney King had been ruthlessly beaten by police officers on a Los Angeles street in 1992, and the video of it was available for all to see. I still remember the brief flood of anger, helplessness, and confusion as the "not guilty" verdict for all the officers involved was read back then. I was working at a public community health center in the heart of South Los Angeles. We nurses, doctors, and medical case workers watched the verdict read on a small TV set in the waiting room as we did our jobs. While disturbed at the injustice, I did not feel the ongoing fire of anger and rage back then like I do now. Truthfully, I do not know why Rodney King's verdict did not hit me as hard as the George Floyd incident. Maybe it was because Rodney King lived while George Floyd died. Perhaps it was because I was not as socially aware as I am now. Possibly it was because I may have internalized some of the negative statements said about Blacks in society early in life, so maybe I was numb. However, although I did not feel the ongoing fire of anger and rage back then, I understood my husband's, family members', and community's anger. I did not condone the LA Rebellion that resulted, but I absolutely understood it.

But this time, on this Monday, May 25, I felt a depth of feelings that I have never felt in my over fifty years of existence. Violence toward us has been a part of Black American existence since we were forced on ships from Africa to the United States. Yet, this George Floyd murder sparked a flame that lingered. The strangulation was so brazen and bold. A grown man begged for almost nine minutes for his own life, even calling on his deceased mother, and yet was still killed. His life was so carelessly taken. Someone who was sworn to protect and serve tossed away a life like he was scraping gum off his shoe.

I remember the burning fire I felt that week—intense emotions that I was unsure if I could rein in. Indignation. Rage. Feeling lost. Disinterest in everything that used to matter. Fear of walking away from it all. Fear at my level of outrage. Uncontrollable crying. Irritability at everyone and everything. Desire to isolate. Insane levels of anxiety. Extreme exhaustion. Stress levels through the roof. Embarrassment that I had not really been present regarding this "stuff" before. Feeling disconnected from others. Feeling a lack of belonging. Hopelessness. A desire to run and go anywhere but here in the United States. Unraveled. Undone. Broken. Shattered. Perhaps you felt this way, too.

I know I am not the only one who felt the flames of overwhelming despair and pain. I am sure that I am not alone in experiencing the fire of ongoing systemic racism. If you are not Black in America but are empathetic with George Floyd's plight (and Breonna Taylor's plight, and Eric Garner's plight...the list goes on), then I can imagine that you feel the pain of social injustice as well. If you are Black in America, I am sure you have your own story of how you felt when you experienced an epiphany regarding the Black experience. I can imagine the pain you felt. The thing about this pain is that it continues. It is ongoing pain, a burning chronic pain that needs to be managed, rather than a one-time acute pain. My question is: how are you handling that pain?

Types of Fire in Our Lives

Pain and fire have much in common. Like fire, pain starts from something that fueled it. It could have begun from the fuel of a traumatic experience or a loss. It could have formed from the fuel of injustice or discrimination. The pain could have been fueled by someone very close to us (through domestic violence or family loss) or someone we did not know (like rape or systemic inequity). Somehow, a chemical reaction occurs between the precipitating event—the fuel—and our perception of it—the oxygen. Like fire, once the pain starts, it does not need much encouragement to continue. Our perceptions can feed into the fire and fan the flames or reduce the fire's intensity. The fire of pain is still there; no one is saying that it isn't. But our perceptions of the pain can increase or decrease the fire's intensity and damage.

Uncontrolled and overwhelming pain will do nothing but consume us and devour us. Like a raging wildfire, unchecked pain can destroy our motivations, drive, will, and esteem. We need help if the fire of pain is too much for us to handle or bear. I hope this book can begin to help because pain is inevitable and universal. None of us can magically avoid pain. Pain is a part of life, and everyone will experience it at some point.

I wrote this book amid the COVID-19 pandemic that affected all parts of the globe. Along with its spread came after-effects—hundreds of thousands of persons dying unexpectedly and prematurely. Millions of lost jobs, lost businesses, and foreclosed homes. Millions of family members grieving over loved ones no longer with them. Dreams were dashed as thousands of those who did survive the virus still live with permanently damaged lungs, barraged kidneys, and weakened hearts. Homes that were financially stable at the beginning of the year were suddenly thrust into a fearful time when financial survival was questionable. Places of worship closed down with windows shuttered and doors locked. Parents worked from home via Zoom while teaching and entertaining children out of school. And we lived with constant uncertainty about the future. Will I get the virus? Will my family or a loved one? Will there be an end to all this? When?

And while the COVID-19 experience has affected everyone, it has been devastating for Blacks in America. For example, the CDC identified the death rate among African Americans as 92.3 deaths per 100,000 persons, which is higher than Hispanic/Latino, white, or Asian persons. Thus, while Blacks in America have a smaller population, they die from COVID-19 in higher numbers than many groups. This means that Black families are being affected severely by COVID-related deaths.

This time of life has been very uncomfortable for many people, and it is outright painful for some. The truth is, there are no guarantees in life that things will permanently stay as they are. We all age and potentially lose some of the youthful vitality we had in our early years. We all have or will experience death and loss of some kind. We all make mistakes and have disappointments, betrayals, accidents, rejections, and embarrassments. We all have the possibility of experiencing health problems or having someone hurt us physically or emotionally. Pain is universal. We need to shine a light on the reality that pain and discomfort meet everyone at their doorstep at one time or another.

However, in addition to the pain that meets everyone at their doorstep, Blacks are disproportionately affected by structural and systemic racism that causes us to die at higher rates at the hands of law enforcement or vigilantes. It is no wonder that there may be many individuals suffering from grief, loss, sadness, depression, anxiety, and trauma in the Black community.

Like fire, pain can sometimes be helpful. What would we do without fire to warm us and cook our food? And pain, controlled, is functional as well. It is a barometer or a thermometer that helps to direct us ("Don't touch that—that's toxic") and warn us. And if we had no sorrow in life, we could not readily appreciate joy. Pain can be a refiner's fire for us. Like fire shapes wood and makes it unrecognizable, pain can help to mold us and shape us into better people—if we allow it to. It can refine us so that which doesn't propel us toward our vision, that which is distracting or useless or wasteful, can be shed in the fire of pain. Pain can purify us if we allow it to.

There is a tool that has helped many to move toward facing their pain and help refine their walk in the fire. That tool is called acceptance and commitment therapy, or ACT for short. It is a psychological intervention that allows us to use our pain to get closer to what we care about and value. This book features tools and exercises to help you on your healing journey. There are also various worksheets available for download at the website for this book, http://www.newharbinger.com /49883, as well as a clinician's guide. If you are willing, let's explore together how ACT may help us navigate the fiery pain of our moments of suffering.

CHAPTER 1

Suffering and the African American Experience

I had no idea that history was being made. I was just tired of giving up.

—Rosa Parks

When I think about the intense pain that overwhelms some of us, I see it as a raging fire, and some are afraid they will be wholly consumed. Sometimes, converging life events are so all-consuming, and the pain is so intense, that a person can feel paralyzed by the pain without any idea of how to get out. The fire of suffering, in these instances, can appear alarming because fire is unpredictable. Fire is difficult to contain. And often, with fire, everything in its wake is left charred, damaged, and sometimes unrecognizable. With no idea about when the fire of pain and suffering will end, or how hot and intense it will get, some folks are just stuck: in too much pain to move, yet too much in pain to stay in pain.

Recovering from trauma in all its forms is something that we desperately need as Blacks in America. As a community, we should know that a therapeutic method exists that can be a culturally embracing framework for us to heal from trauma. Acceptance and commitment therapy (ACT) can be a tool for our pain. When compared with other interventions, such as cognitive behavioral therapy, ACT is relatively new. It was created in 1986 by Steven Hayes, along with Kelly Wilson and Kirk Strosahl (Hayes, Strosahl, Bunting, Twohig, & Wilson 2004). ACT is a useful therapy for several reasons:

It is evidence-based and well-studied, which means a great deal of research shows that it works.

It is a strength-based approach because being diagnosed with something (an anxiety disorder, a depressive disorder, as examples) is not necessary for it to work.

ACT looks at human responses to pain and normalizes the experience of suffering instead of blaming the victim who is experiencing pain.

ACT is an empowering intervention because it helps a person focus on moving toward their own life values.

These qualities of ACT—the non-pathologizing approach, the normalization of the experience of suffering, and the empowering focus on life values—are all characteristics that have been shown in prior research to be culturally appealing to us as Black Americans. ACT is non-pathologizing because you do not need a diagnosis or psychological label in order to use or benefit from ACT. ACT is normalizing because it promotes the view that all humans suffer, not just certain races or other demographics. And ACT is empowering because it focuses on identifying those things that truly matter to us and then moving forward toward them.

Yet, few Blacks utilize ACT. More specifically, few Black clients are offered ACT as a talk therapy choice, and few Black clinicians provide ACT to their clients. Why? There are many reasons. First, less than 5 percent of mental health professionals in the United States are Black. Of those who are clinicians, many have not yet been exposed to ACT training. ACT is not being provided in communities of color on a large scale. And many Black Americans who are hurting are not aware that ACT exists, or that it may be of help to those of us who suffer. Suppose you already had an awareness of ACT before reading this book, and you are Black. In that case, you are one of a few. Thus, this is why this book was written—acknowledging and recovering from trauma in all its forms is something that we desperately need as Blacks in America.

Digging Deeper into the Experience of Pain

Indeed, everyone has experienced grief, sadness, anxiety, or some other feeling of distress. Possibly you have heard of the *Diagnostic and Statistical Manual of Mental Disorders* (DSM), referred to by some as the "clinician's bible" where all psychological diagnoses are categorized (APA 2013). Mental health professionals categorize persons through the DSM because Medicare and Medicaid and other financial sources need a diagnosis (called medical necessity) to provide care. Another reason for the categorization system is to provide a common language among therapists to describe mental health syndromes. But let's hypothesize about this categorization system for a moment and do a "what-if" exercise. Suppose we lump all types of DSM diagnoses (which were socially constructed, by the way) into one general area of suffering.

Then, those "diagnoses" (anxiety disorders, trauma-related disorders, depressive disorders, and so on) would just be different ways of manifesting pain. But how useful are these categorizations to us as individuals who are trying to heal from pain? As John Lewis, the US congressman and civil rights icon, said in 2020:

> Sixty-five years have passed, and I still remember the face of young Emmett Till.... Despite real progress, I can't help but think of young Emmett today as I watch video after video after video of unarmed Black Americans being killed, and falsely accused. My heart breaks for these men and women, their families and the country that let them down—again. (Gallon & Seals 2020)

The pain is real and it does break hearts. What if pain expression was actually on a continuum—instead of a yes or no answer to diagnostic criteria? This discussion regarding the DSM is not coming from a novice; I have been a mental health professional for over two decades, and I have been teaching and training other clinicians on the DSM's specifics for more than ten years. My dissertation chair was one of the most well-known spokespersons regarding the DSM—Dr. Stuart Kirk, distinguished professor emeritus from UCLA. I am not downplaying the utility of the DSM regarding how it works to provide a clinical categorization system. However, when we begin to self-identify with a diagnosis, it creates more problems than solutions.

I will give you an example: The latest version of the DSM, the DSM-5, says that if you have five or more specific depression symptoms for two weeks, you have major depressive disorder. Yet, the book does not differentiate whether that person is depressed in general, or if that person is grieving someone who died recently. A person struggling with depression in all situations is lumped together with a person who just lost their loved one.

You have permission to feel. Everything we go through is not a diagnosis!

Some reactions are normal. It is normal to grieve a loss. It is normal to feel stressed in situations where danger is present. Yet, receiving a diagnosis without a therapist taking your full situation into account can feel stigmatizing. Mental illness is already a taboo subject in our culture. As Blacks, many of us have been negatively labeled in so many ways that receiving a psychological label feels damaging. It feels like unnecessary guilt and shame added to our grief and pain.

However, it is normalizing to know that we need not be ashamed of our pain. All human beings will go through situations or events that cause pain. This is just a normal part of life. Our loved ones die. Sometimes relationships end. Natural disasters happen. Sometimes, we have to make decisions that feel uncomfortable or unfavorable. Pain is a universal human experience—but *suffering* does not have to be.

The Difference Between Pain and Suffering

Even though we may feel alone, ashamed, broken, or defective while going through it, the truth is that pain is familiar to us all. We try to hide that the pain hurts. We try to pretend that we are doing okay with it. We do this because we think that the very presence of pain points a crooked finger at us, accuses us, judges us as weak or limited or incompetent, or not "enough." Because the pain is evidence of that. That is just not true. ACT teaches that *pain is inevitable, while suffering is not.* There is a difference between pain and suffering.

Painful events cause pain. My pastor used to say, for example, "Hurting people hurt other people." And no matter how wise, careful, or sweet we are, we all will experience pain in life.

Suffering, on the other hand, is caused by trying to wiggle away from the pain—trying to squash it, avoid it, self-medicate to dull it, or control it. We all experience pain, but we do not have to experience suffering (Follette & Pistorello 2007). To illustrate this, I will tell two stories.

Story: A Broken Glass

The first is a story about a boy named Marcus. Marcus, age twelve, broke one of his mother's favorite glasses. He dropped it on the kitchen floor and it shattered into many pieces. One of the shards cut his left foot because he was barefoot in the kitchen when he dropped the glass.

There were two ways that Marcus could have handled the situation. Marcus could have immediately told his mother what happened and apologized. He could have asked for help with his foot. If asked, his mother likely would have checked his wound to see if there was any glass still in his foot and carefully removed it. His mother would have probably cleaned the wound (although it would have been painful), added some antibacterial ointment to the injury, and protected the damage with a bandage. His mother would likely have forgiven Marcus's accident and helped clean the glass shards from the kitchen.

However, that was not the way that Marcus handled the situation. Instead, when he dropped the glass and cut his foot, Marcus began to have thoughts. "I broke one of her favorite glasses." "She's gonna hate me for that." "I'm so stupid." "Why can't I do anything right?" "I'm such a loser."

From his thoughts, Marcus began to feel embarrassment, guilt, shame, anxiety, and fear. These feelings were not attached to the pain he was feeling in his foot—these feelings were related to the thoughts he was thinking. Because his thoughts were painful, Marcus decided to hide the situation. He did not tell his mother about the incident. Marcus tried to hide the glass shards so his mother would not know the glass was broken. He covered up his wound by trying to hide it—he put on some socks. He did not clean the wound or put a bandage on it to protect it. Instead, Marcus tried to hide it and not think about it anymore.

Two weeks later, he was in much more pain than he was the day he broke the glass. Marcus had difficulty walking on his left foot. His wound had gotten infected, and dirt accumulated in it. His foot had lots of pain, swelling, and foul-smelling drainage. Marcus had to eventually tell his mother, and they had to go to the hospital, get antibiotic treatment, and lance the abscess that had grown on his foot.

In the first scenario, Marcus felt pain. In the second scenario, Marcus felt additional pain as his shame led him to hide the incident, which caused ongoing suffering.

Story: *From Childhood Pain to Adult Suffering*

Now, let's talk about Jacquie, a twenty-five-year-old Black woman. When she was younger, she went to a junior high where she was one of only a few Blacks. During her junior high years, she was constantly bullied and called the N-word. A handful of students taunted her and called her dirty because of her skin color and made animal noises as she passed. Also, she was sexually abused by a white male student who she found out was just dating her to see what Black girls' privates looked like. Her junior high years were extremely painful, but she tried to deal with them valiantly by ignoring the incidents and being a "good" girl. She did not want to burden her extremely hardworking parents with what was going on at the school. So, she never talked with her family about her experiences, and she never addressed them.

Flash forward to age twenty-five. Jacquie, over the years, has tried to avoid thinking about the situation in junior high. But some words continued to surface in her mind later, long after she graduated from college. "I am less than." "I am not as good because of my race." "I am ugly." "I have to work twice as hard just to be accepted in any environment." "Maybe I am lazy." As a result of her thoughts, she feels ongoing personal shame, guilt, ongoing sadness, anxiety, and fear.

Instead of addressing the pain from being bullied, she tried to avoid those thoughts, and the pain became suffering. Jacquie's thoughts trickled into her relationship choices. She chose abusive, dismissive, rude, or absent men as partners. Painful thoughts leaked into her job choices. She never thought she was good enough to try for the jobs that she really wanted. She began to isolate more, and she shied away from potential friendships. She started to avoid opportunities when they arose. She avoided her pain.

Jacquie tried to make herself feel better through perfectionism, workaholic behavior, hyper-religiosity, legalism, superficiality, and other self-medicating distractions. Way before COVID-19, Jacquie was already wearing a mask in public. It was a mask of her own making—an impenetrable facade as she pretended to be what she thought she should be in public. Instead of facing her racial wound, she hid her pain and pretended that it was not there. Sadly, as a result, Jacquie continues to suffer to this day.

Is All Human Suffering the Same?

It is true that all humans suffer and go through pain. But some individuals have more pain (more intense pain, more frequent pain, or both) thrust upon them via their environments than others. I saw a *USA Today* article that quoted Justin Bieber via Instagram, talking about his own mental health struggles. He said:

> It's hard to get out of bed in the morning with the right attitude when you are overwhelmed with your life, your past, job responsibilities, emotions, your family, finances, your relationships… You start foreseeing the day through lenses of 'dread' and anticipate another bad day. (Yasharoff 2019)

Being famous, young, wealthy, and talented does not preclude anyone from pain. All humans, even famous ones like Justin Bieber, can struggle with pain. However, Justin Bieber's struggle with pain is different from a homeless mother's struggle on Skid Row. Justin Bieber's battle with pain is different from the struggle of a young Black male trying to survive while living in a violent gang-ridden neighborhood. All of the battles are equally valid and equally important to those struggling with them. However, the complex nature of those struggles differs: the intensity, quality, and frequency of the pain. The pain also differs in terms of the percentage of pain that is internally generated versus externally generated. We can create our own pain within, but outside events can also cause us pain.

In general, all humans are affected by certain factors that influence their experience of suffering. Studies show that, universally, we all experience suffering controlled by our genetics, gender, and lifestyles. Our pain is also influenced by our propensity toward depression or anxiety, life stressors, physical health, social factors, fear of pain, beliefs about pain, and past painful experiences. For example, men are often socialized to ignore the pain and refrain from expressing that pain exists (outside of anger or rage). Conversely, women are socialized to talk more freely about pain and express a broader range of emotions without ridicule. This affects men's experience of suffering: they are socially trained to endure pain longer, for fear of being told to "man up" or "stop wussing out." This is why it is more challenging to convince men to obtain medical treatment or psychological treatment. They may live with the pain longer without receiving help and suffer silently.

Here are the factors influencing the experience of suffering:

- genetics

- gender

- lifestyle

- depression or anxiety

- life stress

- long-term health problems

- social factors

- fear of pain

- beliefs about pain

- past pain experiences

However, there are additional factors that influence our experiences as Blacks in the United States. The social determinants of health model adopted by the World Health Organization points to other factors that influence Blacks' experience of suffering.

What are the social determinants of health? They have been described as "the conditions in which people are born, grow, work, live, and age" (CDC 2018). In the United States, these conditions are shaped by the distribution of money, power, and resources at global, national, and local levels. It is evident that money, power, and resources are not equitably distributed in the United States. This unequal distribution affects us as Blacks in America in many ways. One blatant example of this presented while I was writing this book: the varied experience of the millions of individuals with COVID in the United States. President Trump, a rich man, was admitted to the hospital and given three types of COVID-19 treatments, including one not available to the public at the time. In contrast, those in low-income areas had difficulty obtaining testing and did not have the medical insurance or resources necessary to be treated for COVID. Thus, many suffered silently in their homes and or succumbed to the illness and died.

The social determinants of health affect a wide range of health risks and outcomes. The term "determinants" is used because these factors are life-enhancing resources. Our ability to obtain resources (food, housing, money, transportation, education, and health care) determines whether we have poor quality and longevity of life (see Figure 1, Shim et al. 2014).

The Social Determinants of Mental Health

Thus, there is a very complex, integrated, and overlapping influence of social structures and economic systems responsible for most health inequities. These complex conditions have created disparities for Blacks. Research shows that when Blacks in America are in emotional pain, we are:

- less likely to have access to available mental health services

- less likely to receive the necessary mental health care

- significantly underrepresented in mental health research

- often the recipients of inferior quality of treatment, misdiagnosis, and experience cultural bias in care. (NAMI 2020)

In addition to the universal factors, we as Blacks in America also have additional factors that can influence our experience of suffering and pain (Solar & Irwin 2010):

- access to care

- racism and discrimination

- illness chronicity

- socioeconomic status

- life stress

- police and prosecutor bias

- cultural competence

- stigma and cultural distrust

- cultural or spiritual beliefs

- experiences of past pain

Black Americans have more difficulty accessing quality health and mental health care, experience higher rates of chronic stress due to racism and discrimination, fear death for ourselves or our loved ones due to police and prosecutor bias, and have increased levels of cultural distrust of "the system," a system that has been noted to treat some of its citizens (and immigrants) inequitably.

Thus, when answering the question, "Is all suffering the same?," the answer is a definitive no. While all suffering is valid, there are differences in the types, quality, intensity, and frequency of pain experiences that individuals go through. And we as Blacks in America have a high and sometimes unbearable burden of suffering.

Examining Black Pain

In June 2020, over two hundred Black Americans shared what it is like to be Black in America (NPR 2020). Here are a few quotes from various Black Americans. They speak for themselves.

"I'm not going to lie—I am angry. As a Black man in America, it is already hard enough that we have to fight within ourselves to become a better person, but there are countless forces working outside of ourselves that are also working against us and have been for generations."—a Black man

"DNA will continue to scream in agony because Black men and boys are not safe in America. I will try to hold the pain and soul wounds of my people. I will mourn because I know wishes, words or rituals cannot keep my son and grandson alive."—a Black mother, grandmother, and minister

"They are my gentle giants, but they are big Black boys, and I have to remind them that the world doesn't see them as kids, and there is real danger just for existing."—a Black mother of Black teens

"I'm afraid when I get pulled over. My family has served in every war since World War I. They served before Black Americans could vote, and we continue to serve even though we are not always seen as equals. It hurts."—a Black veteran

"It must be nice to wake up in the morning and feel safe, to not be afraid to go out and do what you have to do for the day, to hang out with your friends, not be afraid of the police. I wonder what that is like."—a Black man and new father of a son

"Now here we are in the twenty-first century, and I have a two-month-old grandson, and I wonder if he, as a young Black man, will survive in America. I feel like Black men and women are an endangered species here in America. That's what's it like being Black in America now!"—a Black grandmother whose mother experienced the Ku Klux Klan burning crosses in their yard

These statements clearly show the racial pain and trauma that is presently felt by so many of us as Black Americans. As pressing as this pain is, racial pain is not the only pain that some of us navigate. The accumulated pain—chronic pain, acute pain, microaggressions, blatant and traumatic violence, grief and loss, natural disasters, and relationship issues— results in wear and tear on our systems.

Out of the Fire

There have been many times that I have felt the pain of disappointment, rejection, loss, or physical illness. When at my lowest moments, someone would speak a kind word to me at the right moment that motivated me to get up and get going again. There is a scripture in the Bible that I often meditate on. In fact, it is my personal vision and life's mission statement:

> And of some have compassion, making a difference:
>
> And others save with fear, pulling them out of the fire; hating even the garment spotted by the flesh. (Jude 22–23: KJV)

As I think about these words, I think of our needs as humans. Sometimes in our lives, all we need is a little bit of compassion from someone else: a smile, an encouraging word, a hug, a note of appreciation. A little bit of compassion goes a long way, and just a simple act of kindness toward us can make a tremendous difference in our lives at the right time. It can be the difference between pressing on and moving forward or giving up.

Sometimes we are in such an overwhelming place of pain that it feels as if we are in the midst of the unquenchable fire of pain and suffering. We are in the fire, whatever that fire may be in life. This is when we need more help than just a pat on the back, a kind word, or a compassionate nod. When we're in the fire, we need an actual physical hand, helping us to get out.

Imagine there are two people in a pool, and both of them are brand new swimmers. Person A is swimming like a new swimmer— often holding onto the pool's sides and making mistakes in form and technique while swimming. Person B is drowning. They are flailing their arms, desperately trying to stay afloat, but they are about to go under. For Person A, verbal encouragement is great. But for Person B, verbal encouragement is not just insensitive; it is deadly.

Black Americans have suffered generations of trauma and oppression, yet there have been no clear and concrete evidence-based interventions to address that complex trauma. Hopefully, this book can serve to meet this unmet need. Sadly, so many of us are in the midst of the fire. The fire of fearing for our lives and the lives of our sons, daughters, and loved ones. The fire of police brutality and a system that rewards Black and brown lives' extermination or oppression. It is my hope that this book will serve as a hand outstretched to you and your Black loved ones who are struggling in the fire.

CHAPTER 2

Moving from Fire to Psychological Flexibility

Bringing the gifts that my ancestors gave, I am the dream and the hope of the slave. I rise. I rise. I rise.

—Maya Angelou

One of my loved ones experienced an unexpected and devastating racial injustice in which they were treated as if they were less than a person. The sheer racial injustice of the whole situation was so hard for me to bear. It is distressing to see your loved ones in pain. It is disheartening to see that decisions affecting safety and life or death are not always just or objective. It is demoralizing to feel helpless to do anything about the pain you, a family member, or a loved one experiences when an unjust system enacts racism.

Afterward, I struggled for about a week to process the event. I admit that I had difficulty functioning that week. I would wake up at 3 a.m. night after night. I felt acute anxiety during the day, experiencing agitation, restlessness, exhaustion, problems concentrating, tense muscles, stomach aches, and nausea. I did not feel right.

But that month just happened to be one of the busiest months of my life. I had several products due, including a grant and a publication. I still needed to be available and present to do my job as a professor—teach classes, do teaching prep, and grade. I prayed to just have an hour to stop everything. I wanted to yield to paralysis. I wanted time to grieve and to pout. I wanted time to allow my emotions to wash over me like a wave. But I never got that chance. I survived, and I succeeded, hour by hour, in continuing to move toward what mattered to me despite my pain.

I still taught classes. In fact, a student told me that she enjoyed the course and learned a lot. I was dumbfounded, amazed that I was able to positively influence someone amid my pain. I continued writing the grant, continued being present for my loved one, and continued to produce academically, even during my pain. I realized later that I was actually living out the flexibility and adaptability that lead to the goal of ACT: psychological flexibility. Let's look at these more closely.

Flexibility

When I think of flexibility, I think of a rubber band that can stretch and expand to hold things much larger than it initially looks like it is capable of holding. I think of a child putting water in a balloon and how the child's eyes light up as the balloon gets much bigger and heavier than it was before it was stretched. Flexibility is the quality of bending easily without breaking; the ability to be easily modified; willingness to change or compromise, capable of being flexed; pliant; characterized by a ready capability to adapt to new, different, or changing requirements. Adjustable. Elastic. Fluid. Malleable. Modifiable.

The benefits of flexibility among people are vast, as we saw when the COVID-19 pandemic forced us to apply our flexibility. The pandemic created a time of extraordinary change with hundreds of thousands of lives of loved ones lost. Businesses closed, and weddings, funerals, and graduations were canceled. Schools closed, jobs were lost, and travel was postponed. Homes became workplaces. Living rooms became schools. Roles changed as well: parents became teachers, and nurses and doctors were casualties in precarious positions. Activities that people used to lean on to make them feel better—like going to the gym or socializing—were rare or non-existent. Sadly, many lost homes or apartments and lost jobs, cars, and family members. Some lost physical abilities due to a bout of COVID that they did not recover from. The pandemic is just one example of how uncertainty is at every corner. It showed us how the traits of adaptability and flexibility are essential.

Adaptability

An article in the *Washington Post* described adaptability as the ability to "ride change like a wave" (Heath 2020). I love thinking about the analogy of a wave because we know that even at a wave's highest point, that wave will recede soon enough. And we know that, at our lowest points in life, if we can just hold on, another wave of change is indeed coming. Some changes can certainly be difficult to bear. However, it is how we cope with change—how we ride the wave—that counts. Will we be swallowed up by the tide, or will we surf it? Here is a story of what can happen when we are not able to adapt.

Story: *Being Swallowed by Change*

Reverend Dawson is a sixty-year-old Black male living in South Carolina. He has been a pastor for almost forty years of a mid-sized Baptist church in his community, and he has a wife, four adult children, and ten grandchildren. Over the years, his ministry's quality has been respected in his community and throughout his state. Throughout the decades that he has been a pastor, he poured his passion and efforts into his church and congregants. He took his vocation as a pastor seriously, so much so that sometimes his wife or children felt a bit neglected. Each week took on a very familiar and comforting pattern over the years: Tuesday night Bible study, Wednesday night prayer, Friday night youth meeting, and Sunday services. Although his church was mid-sized, the congregants were active and engaged.

Then COVID-19 happened. Suddenly, his church doors had to close for some time while government restrictions occurred. He knew other pastors had switched to digital congregations on YouTube, Facebook, or other social media platforms. But Reverend Dawson had limited technological knowledge. In fact, he felt very negative about technology and had skepticism about its utility. The church's activities stopped, even his ability to eulogize congregants who died during the pandemic.

Reverend Dawson simply could not think through how to adapt to this COVID-19 change. Besides, Reverend Dawson began to realize that he had not prepared well for retirement as a pastor. He had not set aside enough retirement funds to live a financially comfortable life for himself and his wife.

Reverend Dawson began to sleep for hours during the day and started to isolate himself in his bedroom, away from his wife, adult children, and grandchildren. He stopped taking calls from the church's congregants and fell into a depression. He felt that he just could not adapt to all of the changes that had happened.

With adaptability, unlike Reverend Dawson, you can see possibilities in unanticipated change. Even though it is true that some people are more adaptable by nature than others, it is still possible to grow in this area. The good thing is that we can accept and embrace change, even if we did not do so before. In the *Washington Post* article, Laurie Leinwand stated, "We have to let go of the need to plan from A to Z and learn to be okay with planning from A to B." (Heath 2020).

Adaptability is akin to flexibility, but slightly different. Being adaptable means that you can change despite varied conditions. Being flexible means that you can do this easily. However, if you are *resilient*, you'll be able to withstand or recover quickly from unexpected or difficult situations, adapting to (and often enjoying) change regularly.

Resilience

A word similar to flexibility that has been used to describe African American populations for decades: resilience. Being resilient is defined as being capable of withstanding shock without permanent deformation or rupture; tending to recover from or adjust easily to misfortune or change.

Resilience has been studied in Blacks to determine what factors help African Americans live and function. We have continued to survive despite adversities such as exposure to chronic community violence, disproportionate economic hardship, racial discrimination, and inequitable social structures. There are protective factors (positive coping elements) that help Blacks in America endure. These include extended family systems, spirituality, cultural pride, positive racial socialization, and social support (Jones 2007; Brown 2008).

In fact, African American resilience has been highly researched for decades. One study by Tanya Alim and colleagues looked at trauma, resilience, and recovery in a high-risk African American population. (Alim et al. 2008). They found that one of the most essential factors that differentiated those who had resilience from those who did not was purpose in life. African Americans who have life purpose are much more resilient than those who do not. That is good news because life purpose (in the form of values) is something that the ACT model helps people explore.

However, Dr. Leslie Anderson asks a great question: why are Black families expected to continuously have to adapt to adverse environments (Anderson 2019)? Why do we always have to be resilient? Dr. Anderson discusses that Black families in the United States are often encouraged to demonstrate perseverance amid chronic adversity. Despite continued systematic oppression, we are expected to model resilience. Why are Black families expected (in spoken and unspoken ways) to continuously adapt to adverse environments? I agree with her position that the concept of resilience needs to be reexplored and conceptualized differently when discussing Black families.

There have been Blacks who have described what they think resilience is. One Black woman said, "So, I just call 'making it' living one day at a time, knowing that… your bills are paid, your kids doing all right… You ain't got to be all over the top… trying to get a Mercedes.…I do one day at a time, and eventually, I'm going to get up there…" (Brodsky 1999, 152).

As a Black woman, I don't want to move toward resilience in my life. Resilience, to me, is to endure, to keep surviving despite suffering. Yes, resilient people keep moving despite adversity. But resilience does not speak about the internal process that these individuals go through. They may be physically moving forward in their behaviors, yet they may be experiencing an emotional or mental toll.

I applauded Dr. Anderson's statement when she said that we, as a nation, bear the responsibility to do more than just encourage resilience in Black families. We also have the responsibility to intentionally work toward ending the conditions that necessitate resilience in the first place (Anderson 2019). Instead of moving toward resilience, I want to move toward flexibility. Flexibility is better. Becoming more flexible is more courageous because it allows us to face our pain. It is more freeing because it allows us to move forward in our values during pain instead of being reactive.

Psychological Flexibility

Many years ago, I was in prayer and I realized that, spiritually, I was not like the name that I was given at birth. My mother named me Jennifer. I looked up what the word "Jennifer" meant and found out that it means "white wave." White wave, to me, represents instability and wavering. But my spirit, the essence of who I am, is not like a "Jennifer." Instead, my soul is more like the legendary phoenix. The phoenix is a mythical bird from Greek mythology that submits to being enveloped in fire every five hundred years. The fire does not consume the phoenix, however. Instead, the phoenix is reborn and transformed through the fire. So, in my life journey, I have been learning how to not only yield to fire (fire of pain, tribulation, hurts, disappointments) but also learn how to dance amid the fire. Thus, my spirit, the essence of who I am, is more like a phoenix than a white wave. When I think about psychological flexibility, I think of others who are also learning how to dance in the fire and move toward their values during pain.

Psychological flexibility, a term used in ACT, is the ability to be fully aware of today and right now. Even if today and right now are painful. And, with awareness, a psychologically flexible person can move toward the most meaningful things to them. (Hayes, Strosahl, & Wilson 2012). It is being able to come in full contact with painful experiences, and even while doing so, to consciously choose to move toward our values—toward a life that is meaningful for us, despite the pain we feel. In other words, how closely can we stay in the present while at the same time being aware of all of our thoughts and emotions? Can we just be mindful of them without trying to run from them, control them, or change them? And can we move forward in our hopes and dreams despite them? (Moran 2015, 26).

The wonderful thing about psychological flexibility is that people can learn how to increase their levels of flexibility. In fact, increasing psychological flexibility is the whole aim of ACT. It is absolutely possible for those struggling to address the pain they are in to move from a place of suffering to a place of movement and action. It would have been wholeheartedly possible for Reverend Dawson to move from paralysis and isolation to actively engage with the family he loves and participate in activities meaningful to him.

ACT is an evidence-based practice. That means several high-quality research studies have been done that show that ACT works. ACT has been shown to increase psychological flexibility in those who receive ACT therapy. The opposite of psychological flexibility, psychological inflexibility, has been associated with more significant psychological problems (depression, anxiety, and other conditions). The higher a person's psychological flexibility, the lower their scores will be on psychopathology measures. The more psychologically flexible they are, the higher their scores will be on quality-of-life scales.

Psychological flexibility is actually freedom-speak. Being able to experience pain, yet not allowing the pain to dictate how our lives go—that is freedom. As Blacks, we greatly value freedom, mainly because our history shows how limited our freedom has been. With the Emancipation Proclamation of 1863, enslaved persons were declared free. But they were not legally free until two years after the Confederacy's defeat, learning the news from Union soldiers, other enslaved people, or (sometimes months later) their enslavers.

And even after "emancipation," what has freedom looked like over the years? True freedom can appear elusive to many African Americans. Statistics from 2016 show that:

- African Americans own about one-tenth of the wealth of white Americans.

- The Black-white wealth gap has not recovered from the Great Recession of 2008.

- Blacks are more likely to experience adverse income shocks, but are less likely to have emergency savings.

- Blacks face systematic challenges in narrowing the wealth gap with whites. This gap persists regardless of households' education, marital status, age, or income (Hanks, Solomon & Weller 2018).

Thus, much work is to be done regarding freedom and equity for all in the United States. Yet, even while that work is incomplete, our pain experiences should not be allowed to entirely govern our behavior. We deserve to be free—physically, mentally, and spiritually. We deserve to enjoy a quality of life right now, rather than waiting until all systemic issues are fixed. A pastor I had would always say to his congregants, "Don't let anyone live rent-free in your head." We tend to give so much power, at times, to our own emotions, to other people's statements, and to circumstances and events in our lives. And when we avoid the feelings that these painful thoughts or circumstances produce, we give them more power instead of less power. By trying to blow our flames out, we actually fuel them.

Have you ever tried to blow out candles on a birthday cake and were unsuccessful the first (and maybe second) time? When you blow on the fire, you actually give the fire energy to increase. It takes additional effort for you to blow the fire out. What is the best way to make a candle's fire go out? The best way is to snuff it out by robbing it of additional fuel for energy—cutting off its air supply.

This is how the fire of pain fuels itself. We feel pain, and sometimes we "blow" on it—we stretch it, speak on it, massage it, and add energy to it by reacting to its presence. Or we try to hide from it, evade it, distract from it, and the fire gets more prominent as a result. Thus, both anxiety and avoidance play roles in how effectively or ineffectively we can navigate our own painful experiences.

Anxiety

Like sadness, anxiety is an unpleasant but normal and functional experience. It can helpfully provide us with warning signs about perceived threats to our safety and well-being. We all are built to respond to danger. Our bodies have been programmed to have a fight-or-flight response mechanism that protects and preserves them in the face of danger. It is an adaptive function placed in us for the sole purpose of self-preservation. When we experience a real danger or threat, the fight-or-flight response kicks in: adrenaline and other chemicals are activated. Physical symptoms occur such as rapid heart rate, palpitations, increased blood pressure, and sweating. In a dangerous situation, our minds also have a normative reaction: our focus narrows on the danger and we become laser-focused on it. We might even experience the world differently as a result. Some describe how they perceived their surroundings during a dangerous or traumatic event. Some state, "Time… it felt slower…Time stood almost still," or "Everything else was foggy and out of focus," or "It felt surreal like I was in a movie." For instance, when individuals experienced September 11 in New York, Katrina in New Orleans, or the major wildfires in California, their anxiety response in those situations helped them stay alive. All of this is functional behavior when there is a real danger. However, anxiety becomes dysfunctional in certain circumstances. It becomes a problem when:

- It creates a sense of powerlessness or an inability to act or produces a level of self-obsession that interferes with our problem-solving.

- The fight-or-flight response is triggered in situations where there is no real danger or when it creates doubt about reality's nature.

- Our response to threat produces a chronic and exhausting state of alertness where the flight or fight response is always turned on, even when there is no physical danger.

- Avoidance becomes chronic or perpetual. When avoidance continues to happen, we may behave as if we are threatened when we may not actually be in danger.

During dangerous or unsafe situations, our behavior gets narrow and rigid for good reason. But if we are no longer in danger and our behavior stays inflexible, we can develop a self-protective stance that could damage us. Here is how this happened for Rob.

Story: *Feeling in Permanent Danger*

Rob was a twenty-eight-year-old Black male who happened to be in the wrong place at the wrong time. He was sitting in a car, talking to a male cousin he had not seen for a while. The police pulled up behind the car and asked him and his cousin to step out of the vehicle. Unknown to him, his cousin had drugs in the car, so both men were arrested.

Rob did not have money for an attorney, so a public defender was appointed to his case. Unfortunately, his public defender was overcommitted at best, uninvolved and unconcerned at worst. Thus, when Rob stood in front of a judge known to be "hard on crime," the judge threw the book at him and gave him the maximum sentence. Rob ended up spending over nine months in prison for what should have been a misdemeanor offense.

While Rob was in prison, he had to protect himself and show others that he was not a punk. He had to assert himself and be tough. Rob quickly learned how to create an intimidating presence. He soon became one of the relatively respected inmates in prison due to his ability to fight and intimidate.

In about nine months, he was released. Although he was out physically, he was not out mentally. He continued with his "game face," intimidation tactics, and aggression to protect himself. Protecting himself sometimes took the form of being aggressive toward his girlfriend and his children. Sometimes he acted out physically and was abrupt. If Rob was asked, he would say that he loved his girlfriend and children and truly valued their relationship. Yet, he no longer could be vulnerable with anyone. Rob is on the verge of losing his girlfriend and damaging his relationship with his children. However, he does not know how to stop the rigid behavior pattern that he finds himself continuing.

If I were Rob's therapist and had the opportunity, I would love to ask Rob a few questions. I would like to find out, "Is every situation in your life unsafe now?"

Yes, police brutality happens, the court system is unjust at times, and prison is unsafe. But what about now that he is out? Are his children safe? Is his girlfriend safe? And if so, is treating them as dangerous moving him toward what he values—a close relationship with them? Hopefully, Rob would be open to thinking about these things. Rob needs psychological flexibility. He needs the ability to differentiate dangerous situations from situations that are not dangerous.

As African Americans, we have situations that cause us ongoing trauma, absolutely. The fear that our family members, or even we, might be targeted erroneously for police brutality or even death is a reality. The frustration at a criminal justice system that is not always fair in distributing sentences is real. The possibility of living with microaggressions or even outright racism in housing situations, employment settings, and educational systems is valid. So, for Black Americans, psychological flexibility may begin with the ability to discern the difference between real danger and subjective danger. Physical danger requires strategies that emotional danger does not.

Avoidance

When you think about how avoidance looks for Blacks, you see that some avoidance may be self-protective. Just like a child should avoid crossing the street without looking both ways, some of us have taught our children how to act when the police stop us. "Don't confront them." "Keep your hands where they can be seen." "Watch your tone of voice." "Stay humble!" Many who have followed that advice have still died due to police or vigilante violence, even with home training. So, sadly, we often do feel that fight-or-flight response when we see a police car behind us flashing its lights. Perhaps our heart does beat faster, and we search in our minds for some way to escape. Avoidance can be very complicated for Blacks in America.

However, ACT teaches us how to live our best life within the circumstances we presently find ourselves in. Can we evaluate and identify the safe spaces in our lives? Can we become aware of those relationships and nourishing activities that we value and are not damaging? For those settings, avoidance only hinders—it never helps.

What Can We Do to Have More Psychological Flexibility?

How can we begin to heal? How can we address the past and present trauma we have suffered as African Americans? Is it possible for us to move away from rigid ways of thinking and move forward in our purposes despite our pain? ACT may be a way for us to move toward healing. As Steven C. Hayes wrote, we can pivot toward what matters to us: "Pain and purpose are two sides of the same thing. A person struggling with depression is very likely a person yearning to fully feel. A socially anxious person is very likely a person yearning to connect with others. You hurt where you care, and you care where you hurt." (Hayes 2020)

As the originator of ACT, Hayes proposed a model to improve psychological flexibility. The model has six core components to it and is thus called a hexaflex (*hexa* is Greek for the number six and "flex" refers to flexibility). The six core processes of the model are:

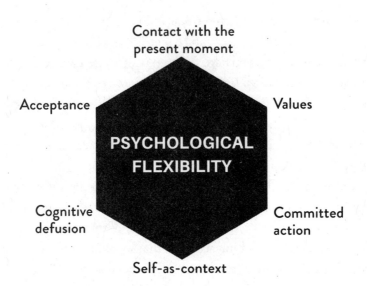

These six areas are positive psychological skills that can be developed in treatment with an ACT-practicing therapist or through self-help exercises. Taken as a whole, each of these processes supports the other, and all target psychological flexibility. You can learn about one or all of them in no particular order, as we'll explore in chapter 9. They all come together to help us move from being stuck emotionally toward actively doing what we genuinely want to do in life.

While I have over thirty years of experience as a counselor and therapist, I had not heard about ACT until much later—only within the past few years. A colleague who does mindfulness work mentioned it to me a few years ago. I began to do a Google search on the intervention. I then signed up for introductory three-day training on ACT. I was the only Black therapist in a room filled with therapists. But after I heard about the concepts of this intervention and what they targeted, I was hooked. As a therapist and researcher doing life while Black in America, I began to think about the six core concepts of ACT in more detail. I love this intervention, but I wondered why I (and many other Black therapists) had not heard about it earlier.

A couple of years ago, I offered a training on ACT geared toward African American clinicians. The room was packed, so much so that people were standing in the hallways looking in. One of the first questions I asked the primarily Black clinical audience was, "How many of you have heard of ACT before this training?" Only two people raised their hands in the room. This is often the reception that I get when speaking about ACT to clinicians of color. Most of them were unaware of ACT before I discussed it. I was saddened and a bit angry at the fact that few Black clinicians were aware of this evidence-based practice because I saw how ACT could facilitate healing African American trauma.

As an intervention, ACT has some benefits that may be appealing to the African American population. First, ACT shows potential in treating trauma for Black Americans because it is a non-pathologizing approach (McLean & Follette 2016). That means that there is no stigma attached to getting help with ACT because you don't need a label or diagnosis to use it. Other methods have the goal of the reduction of symptoms. For instance, cognitive behavioral therapy aims to reduce depressive, anxious, or other negative thoughts. To use interventions like cognitive behavioral therapy, you first have to be diagnosed or shown that you have a problem—too many depressing thoughts, too many anxious thoughts. Often, a person needs to receive a diagnosis (a label) such as major depressive disorder or generalized anxiety disorder. Only then can the therapist begin to reduce the behaviors and thoughts associated with the diagnosis.

But, ACT is different: you do not have to have a diagnosis to begin work. Instead, ACT promotes that suffering is part of being human for all humans, not just certain "weak" people. Everybody has pain. Everybody suffers. ACT normalizes suffering, normalizes pain, and normalizes avoidance as normal human responses. At the same time, ACT helps individuals move toward more value-driven living. Based on prior research, African Americans do not want to be treated in therapy as being lacking or pathological. As a race, we already suffer so much negative stigma that we do not want to be doubly stigmatized in treatment.

Something is soothing and normalizing in realizing that pain is just a part of life for all humans. It is not an outlier—it is a normal part of life. We as African Americans need strength-based approaches like ACT to heal.

As I mentioned before, though, I began to think about the six core concepts of the hexaflex regarding Black pain and how to present them to my clients. The hexaflex core concepts—acceptance, contact with the present moment, values, committed action, self-as-context, and cognitive defusion—were very useful in content. However, each term was abstract and difficult to present in ways that my clients could solidly grasp. So, I engaged in reframing the hexaflex in terms more relatable to the African American community. Thus, culturally embracing replacement terms were developed. "Contact in the present moment" was changed to "In the here and now." "Values" was changed to "Living life like its golden." "Committed action" was changed to "Getting it done." "Acceptance" was changed to "It is what it is." "Self-as-context" was changed to "I am more than my experiences." And "cognitive defusion" was changed to "freedom to let go."

What emerged was an ACT hexaflex model that I felt good about sharing with African Americans.

ACT Hexaflex: POOF Healing

In the Here and Now (Present-Moment Awareness)

**It Is What It Is
(Acceptance)**

**Living Life Like It's
Golden (Values)**

PSYCHOLOGICAL
FLEXIBILITY

**Freedom to Let Go
(Cognitive Defusion)**

**Getting It Done
(Committed Action)**

I Am More Than My Experiences (Self As Context)

This culturally tailored ACT model—POOF (Pulling Out Of Fire)—has surface structure changes to the classic ACT model including language changes, culturally relevant metaphors, and reality-based experiential exercises. The POOF model also incorporates some deep structural changes to the traditional ACT model. For instance, African American stigma and cultural views about mental health treatment are addressed. Racism and discrimination, a significant issue affecting many African Americans, is also addressed (Castro, Barrera Jr., & Holleran Steiker 2010).

This book serves as an introductory exploration of each of the six core ACT processes that may lead us closer to psychological flexibility. Each chapter addresses one of these six core processes. Just briefly, as we look at each of these six areas on the POOF hexaflex, we can ask ourselves the following questions:

- In the here and now: Can you genuinely live now? Or do you find yourself stuck in the past or worrying about the future?

- Living life like it's golden: Like Jill Scott's song, are you living a golden life? Are you living what matters to you?

- Getting it done: is what you are doing getting you where you want to be?

- It is what it is: are you actively avoiding pain in self-damaging ways?

- I am more than my experiences: do you see yourself as your struggle or more than that?

- Freedom to let go: are you stuck or unable to let go?

The following chapters will detail each of these core processes of the ACT hexaflex, exploring them from an African American perspective. It is my hope and prayer that, as you journey through these pages, you will find that some of these concepts can lead toward healing for you and your loved ones.

CHAPTER 3

"It Is What It Is"— Acceptance

Not everything that is faced can be changed, but nothing can be changed until it is faced.

—James Baldwin

I vividly remember a time in my life when I knew I needed emotional healing, but I was struggling. I was married to the love of my life and we had two very young daughters at the time. Unfortunately for us all, my loved one's drug habit detrimentally affected us. There were continual arguments about items suddenly missing from home, people leaving for days without a word, and the financial burden of caring for the family alone was real.

It was an excruciating time for me. The pain of rejection washed over me and pain in the forms of rage and shock enveloped me. Confusion and self-doubt waged war over me each time my loved one tried to convince me that nothing was wrong, saying, "It's your mind playing tricks on you." Fear and despair settled in as abusive effects escalated.

During that time of life, I numbed myself from the pain I was feeling. I minimized it, shrunk it down in my mind to pretend that it didn't exist. "Oh, they didn't mean that [painful action]." "What [painful statement] they said to me was not that bad." "I am making too big a deal out of their [painful] behavior toward me."

I became a master of minimization. I told myself it all was not really that bad. But I began to realize that when I numbed myself to the pain—when I minimized it or rationalized it or legitimized it—I numbed other parts of me as well. Instead of living life in multi-color, I began to see only Black and white and gray. Instead of feeling joy in joyous times, I felt nothing most times. And instead of seeing myself as a whole person, I began to see myself as a caricature of myself. In other words, I saw myself as a cheap and phony knockoff imitation of myself.

I lost myself somewhere. As long as I avoided and minimized and delegitimized my pain, I was not truly living. And eventually, to heal, I had to face my truth and admit that neither my loved one, nor I, for that matter, were healthy. In order for things to change, I had to accept the fact that *it is what it is*. If I never faced the truth about what it was, I would be in a continual loop, going in circles of self-denial, and never genuinely healing.

By avoiding my feelings about my own experience, I unwittingly kept myself stuck in pain. Only when I faced and *accepted* my feelings could I change my situation. What is acceptance in ACT? Acceptance actively allows things and experiences—good or bad, internal or external—to *just be*. Acceptance is not trying to change, control, manipulate, or wish these things into something they are not (Stoddard & Afari 2014). Acceptance in this context is an action word. It means to actively face events that feel negative or uncomfortable for us without trying to change those events or avoid them.

Adverse events like the ones just described may have you stuck in your own life. Events like these may have gotten in the way of you moving forward toward things that matter to you. Acceptance is to be willing to face the private events that happen to you, good or bad, with all five senses. Acceptance is to be aware in the midst of painful moments, to feel them, and to remember them.

Why is this important? Because of the central assumptions of acceptance and commitment therapy (Recovery Research Institute 2020):

1. All humans, regardless of race or any other factor, tend to avoid negative inner (or outer) experiences. That's just human nature.

2. Behavior change happens if you are clear about your values and commit to them.

3. We can be fully aware of a feeling without fighting the feeling.

The assumption here is that only by being courageous enough to face and to come in contact with our whole experience (the good, the bad, the beautiful, and the ugly about our lives) can we live a whole, value-driven life. Avoiding our pain has consequences.

When I was a small child, I used to think that there was a monster in the closet at night and that monsters were in the shadows. But when

I opened the closet door and shined a light in that darkness, I realized that the giant monster was just a coat on a hanger.

Unlike the monster, our pain is real. Our suffering is real. But when we try to avoid thinking about it, when we stuff it down or minimize it, somehow it grows bigger in the shadows. Our anxiety becomes BIG, and our sadness becomes BIG, and our trauma, racial or otherwise, becomes BIG. Big enough to paralyze us and keep us from moving forward toward our dreams.

Once we become willing to shine a flashlight on our pain, we notice that yes, it is still there; yes, it is a legitimate pain; but no, it does not have to control us or stop us from our own goals and dreams. That flashlight is acceptance.

The term acceptance can have different meanings for different people. In ACT, though, acceptance means a willingness to come into contact with our whole life experience, including the nasty inside "stuff" that shows up (Gordon, Borushok, & Polk 2017). Language is often up for interpretation. The term "acceptance" has different meanings and connotations for different people.

What Healthy Acceptance Is Not

It took me some time to realize that "acceptance" in ACT was not the concept of "acceptance" I was taught growing up. For me as an African American woman, the word had negative connotations. Before learning ACT, when I thought of the term, I thought of consenting to something offered, even if that offering was not what I wanted. Accepting, for me, meant agreeing to the status quo. It meant putting up a white flag and surrendering a fight, whatever that fight was. Submission, as an act of giving in to the authority or control of another person or institution, came to mind.

For oppressed groups, the concept of acceptance might seem impossible, unpalatable, and almost cruel. I know the thinking: "I have gone through generations of pain, suffering, and oppression. My trauma is multilayered, and within it is a systematic racial trauma that persists and has persisted for decades. Are you asking me to accept my circumstances? How can you dare to ask me to come in contact with a pain that never leaves?" So, we feel incredulous at the thought of acceptance, rejecting the idea altogether. However, acceptance in ACT is not sadistic. Acceptance is not:

- succumbing to the belief that negative thoughts or actions are okay

- resignation, learned helplessness, or submission

- asking us to get in touch with our pain just as an exercise of futility

There is both a rationale and a function for making contact with the pain. The goal, hope, or prayer for you is to live a life that is meaningful to *you*. To live a life that matters to you. Facing the pain helps you realize that the pain is not in charge of you—you are. And facing the pain can actually become a courageous, empowering act. If we as Blacks could face the pain (childhood trauma, tragedy, and even racial pain) to get to a place where we no longer allow the pain to limit, shackle, or bind us, then true personal freedom can result.

What Is Important to You?

What causes us pain usually points toward what is important to us. Let's think about this concerning racial trauma for a moment. Many Blacks suffer from what is called "racial battle fatigue," a theoretical framework coined by the critical race theorists William Smith and colleagues. It is the cumulative stress, layer on top of layer, of responding to distressing race-related conditions. These stress responses emerge from continually facing racially dismissive, demeaning, insensitive, or hostile racial environments and individuals. Many harmful social, psychological, and physiological stress reactions result, including "frustration; anger; exhaustion; physical avoidance; psychological or emotional withdrawal; escapism; acceptance of racist attributions; and resistance; verbally, nonverbally, or physically fighting back" (Smith, Allen, & Danley 2007).

Fighting racism is so painful because living a life of freedom and equal opportunity matters to most (if not all) of us. When George Floyd died, it caused heart-wrenching pain in many of us in the United States and worldwide. Why? Because human beings matter regardless of skin color. But, George Floyd was not treated with human decency. It hurts us because freedom for all people should matter to us:

> We hold these truths to be self-evident, that all men are created equal, that they are endowed by their Creator with certain unalienable Rights, that among these are Life, Liberty and the pursuit of Happiness. That to secure these rights, Governments are instituted among Men, deriving their just powers from the consent of the governed.

This was stated in the Preamble of the Declaration of Independence. Yet, many of us in the United States do not feel we have the freedom described in this declaration. Thinking about George Floyd and those who died before and after him, in the manner they died, causes pain because equity matters to us. It hurts because feeling safe and feeling treated as Americans (with all the rights and privileges) is essential to our families and us.

These things that cause us racial pain should not be. "Acceptance" does not mean we passively accept racism. But the fact that these issues cause some people pain shows that they are strong values for those who feel that pain. Where we feel pain shows us where we care.

The Cost of Avoiding Pain

When we don't accept our pain, and avoid it, our own thoughts can become internal bullies. Our thoughts push us around, like a critical coach who stands on the sidelines, giving very negative feedback: "That was stupid," "I bet others are doing much better," "You deserved that," or "There is no hope for you." Maybe this originates from within. Or perhaps this came from external sources. Our family members looking down on us. The media saying that being Black is wrong. Continuous microaggressions saying that we are not enough.

In a racially charged age, we try so desperately to distract ourselves from pain via television, food, social media, drugs, relationships—the list goes on. We have become masters at tucking away unwanted thoughts and uncomfortable feelings. For instance, when we experience a racial slight or a microaggression, sometimes we try to avoid it or push it away. Sometimes this is protective, for fear that we might go off. For fear that we might react in rage. For fear that we might lose it all.

But other times, we live in a state of zombie-like existence, moving through life on automatic pilot. In our minds, we minimize the pain, but our body responds to it. We respond with tension, stress, back and neck pain, high blood pressure, and other physical ailments.

Can we instead courageously face our pain and discomfort? Can we face unwanted thoughts without evaluating them or trying to change them? Some ways of thinking may indeed need to change eventually. But can we, at first, become "woke"? In Black culture, there is a term to be "woke," which refers to being awake and not asleep. It has been used to refer to being alert to injustice in society, especially racism. Martin Luther King Jr. gave a commencement address called "Remaining Awake Through a Great Revolution" in 1965. He stated that there is nothing more tragic than sleeping through a social revolution. Some African Americans embrace the term "woke," while others dislike it. However, many of us understand the term, whether we use it or not. But what does it mean to live woke in general? To live wholly woke, not just about race but about everything? To be aware of what is going on around us, positive or negative?

We can pay attention to the *experience* of having painful thoughts like "There must be something wrong with me" rather than focusing on their *meaning*. We can pay attention, rather than deny that the elephant in the room is there. The elephant is right there in the room. Can we first acknowledge that?

Can we begin to be willing to sit with, experience, and notice our frustrations, anger, fatigue, excitement, boredom—whatever is happening with us? A commitment to noticing is just that: a promise to see. It is not a commitment to fix it; it is not a commitment to do something, behave in a certain way, judge, or assess it. It is merely a commitment to be willing to notice and to observe.

The Struggle for Control

Sometimes, we get wrapped up in attempts to control, and we begin to try to control things that were not meant to be controlled. When we feel pain, we attempt to control it. To apply willpower, strength, and endurance to it. To approach the pain with our mind and rationality. To cling to traditions and ritualized behaviors and teachings to avoid facing it. We get busy. We start planning, devising, moving, acting, and working to control the pain. And like an individual with obsessive-compulsive disorder, we spend much of our day deflecting thoughts about the pain. Or instead, we engage in behaviors that we think will reduce the pain such that we do not have time for genuinely living life itself.

The Twelve Steps of Alcoholics Anonymous, which originated from Bill Wilson and his doctor, Bob Smith, in 1935, are known worldwide. The first step of the twelve is powerful, and if you place a blank where the word "alcohol" is, the first step is quite profound for anyone: "We admitted we were powerless over [fill the blank]—that our lives had become unmanageable" (Twelve Steps and Twelve Traditions 1989). This first step toward liberation via the twelve steps is admitting a lack of control. If I were to put that in ACT terms, I would ask, "All that you have been doing to solve your situation…How is that working for you?"

Indeed, from an evolutionary standpoint, we all, as humans, have an innate desire to control. That desire, when used correctly, has helped us to survive. But it's a problem when we have to be in control to get through life. It becomes all about control. After all, maybe you are the competent one who holds the family, job, or the world together while others in your life are not doing their part. So, you start trying to control the people and situations in your life and your feelings about them. Sure, you mean well sometimes. You are trying to be a good girl, good boy, good citizen, good parent, or good child. It is hard to believe that your well-meaning efforts at trying desperately to control your situations have contributed to, rather than alleviated, your anxiety.

Like many, if not all of us, you have experienced pain and suffering. Based on that pain, you may feel that you have to protect yourself from getting hurt again. You have to be in control; you have to be on guard. Thus, you walk around with tense, tight shoulders and a strained jaw, waiting for the other shoe to drop. You never relax from that protective stance, fearing that the same hardships in life and disappointments will happen again if you do not stay on guard. Do you feel:

- as if you cannot relax, for fear that something might go wrong?

- like the world is on your shoulders?

- if you don't carry the weight of the world on your shoulders, everything will fall apart?

If so, you are engaged in continued personal striving. The root definition of the word *striving* means "to quarrel, contend, fight, devote serious effort or energy, to struggle in opposition." We strive personally so much.

The desire for personal control is even more prominent in those who feel they do not have much control over external circumstances. For instance, regarding wealth in America:

African American families have a fraction of the wealth of white families, leaving them more economically insecure and with far fewer opportunities for economic mobility. African Americans have less wealth than whites. Less wealth translates into fewer opportunities for upward mobility. It is compounded by lower income levels and fewer chances to build wealth or pass accumulated wealth down to future generations. (Center for American Progress 2020)

The desire for control is even more prominent for those who have not had much power. As a result of the lack of power, historically, we as Blacks have experienced oppression, suffering, and trauma. The terms "historical trauma" and "intergenerational trauma" come to mind; the unaddressed trauma resulting from the time that Africans were brought to America, including decades of slavery, oppression, and racism. These painful experiences resulted from African Americans having limited external control of their own circumstances. Post-Traumatic Slave Syndrome, as defined by Dr. Joy DeGruy, is a condition that exists due to centuries of chattel slavery, followed by institutionalized racism and oppression. DeGruy said, according to research, trauma is trapped in DNA and can thus be passed down through generations. This resulted in multigenerational adaptive behaviors—some positive reflecting resilience, and others that are harmful and destructive. Many of these behaviors mimic those of PTSD and can include difficulty concentrating, feeling jumpy or being easily irritated, appearing emotionally numb (also called "vacant esteem"), feeling hopeless or depressed, or having a general self-sabotaging outlook (DeGruy Leary & Robinson 2005).

Some are irritated at such a concept as "post-traumatic slave syndrome." Some individuals have asked, "Why don't people get on with their lives?" Others have said, "Slavery was a long time ago. It has nothing to do with today…Some individuals are just using slavery as an excuse not to move forward." However, it is interesting to consider that no trauma therapy was ever offered to descendants of those experiencing the trauma of slavery. Thus, how is it expected that trauma is resolved without intervention or treatment? The Holocaust was an atrocious period, a horrendous time of systematic murder and torture.

It was horrible; it was offensive; it was unconscionable; it was traumatic. That horrific time occurred between 1941 and 1945, and it forever affected the Jewish community. Slavery in America was also an atrocious period for people in America of African descent, and lynching, torture, forced labor, separation of families, rape, and degradation were common during slavery and afterward. Slavery lasted from 1619 to 1865—hundreds of years. And racism, discrimination, and inequity have not stopped—1619 to the present day—over four hundred years of some degree of pain and suffering. Thus, having control can appear like freedom to some. Some Blacks may say, "If I cannot control my environment, then at least I can try to control my internal environment." "I can keep my thoughts and feelings in check." "I can numb myself from all of this pain."

Thus, asking you to stop trying to control your emotions and thoughts might be a big ask. The word "acceptance" might be a big pill to swallow. It might be difficult to convince you to trust the process and commit to acceptance. Even though acceptance is the very thing that will free you to live your life according to your own values.

Story: *Stepping toward Healing*

Jaden, age seventeen, is very fearful and anxious about her life right now. She is called a "transitionally aged youth," which means that she has been in foster care and is about to be on her own at age eighteen. Jaden has a long history of being bounced from foster home to foster home because of her behavior. Since age twelve, she has been in seven foster homes and two group homes, and her present group home is very much ready for her to leave at eighteen.

Jaden has always had a difficult time bonding with foster families. For one, she often felt guilty (as if she was betraying her mom) if she liked a foster parent. And always, at some point, either the foster parent or another kid in the home would say something negative about her mother, and she would lose it. "You don't f——ing say anything negative about my mom! Who the hell are you to talk about my mom?" She would begin raging, physically and verbally fighting the foster parent or kid who said something, destroying property, breaking everything around her in a blind rage. She had been to many therapists and didn't trust any of them, especially when they started asking about her mom. "My mom's a saint. You can't say s— about her!" When the therapists would ask why she and her sibling were in foster care for so long, she would shut down and quickly stop talking to each therapist.

But now, at age seventeen and facing emancipation, Jaden is starting to wonder if she might need to face the painful truth about her mom. Her mom was unable to take care of her and her siblings. Even now, her mom will probably not be there for her to support her as an adult. As painful as this truth was to her, Jaden realized that this is the mother she has. She has an imperfect mom that she still loves, but who cannot support her the way she needs. This was Jaden's first step toward healing. "My mother's ability to be a mother is what it is," she said to herself.

Perhaps like Jaden, you may be going through an excruciatingly painful time right now. The question is: can you get to a place where you are facing it, not by gritting your teeth and having uncontrollable tears and panic in your eyes? Can you yield to a healing process that will get you to a place where you can face the truth of your situation, observe it, and look at it to recognize it for what it is? Only then will you be able to take healthy actions regarding it. Only after acknowledging it can you either explore ways to improve it or learn how to let go.

The Myth of Strength

To get to a place of acceptance, sometimes we as African Americans need to first address stigmas and cultural myths contrary to acceptance. One of the prevalent myths of Black culture includes the myth that we are strong and that we can take high levels of abuse. In a positive sense, we have been seen as resilient (Alim et al. 2008). Resilient individuals adapt more successfully to adversity than non-resilient ones. They are said to cope better with disadvantageous and injurious situations.

However, the myth is that we are stronger as a people. That we can take and endure pain. That we have a higher pain tolerance. This myth is believed and is acted upon in the medical industry ("Don't give them more pain pills—give them less") (Campbell & Edwards 2012). It is believed in our own families. It is perpetrated and passed down from mothers' mouths to their children. It is thought that we can endure depression or anxiety or other mental states longer. As Dr. Rheeda Walker points out in her book, *The Unapologetic Guide to Black Mental Health*:

> The belief that we can endure anything is both a strength and a weakness of our current culture. Those who are having the hardest time can be the least likely to ask for help because they are afraid of not appearing "Black enough." This happens on top of everything else that is causing pain.

In addition, the myth of strength affects each gender in different ways.

The Strong Black Woman

Many of us claim, with reverence, an identity that revolves around strength: the strong Black woman. The strong Black woman schema includes behaviors such as emotional suppression, self-reliance, and caregiving. However, the strong Black woman schema has also been linked to negative outcomes like anxiety, depression, and binge-eating for African American women.

Along with that identity is an idea that martyrdom is right, that sacrificing oneself for our families is good. That myth involves the belief that Black women are tireless and invulnerable. That myth has created unrealistic burdens at home, in the workplace, and elsewhere.

There are two mantras that are incongruent about Black women. On the one hand, the mantra is "Black women are undeserving." They are unworthy of public assistance; they are unworthy of sympathy. They are unworthy of equal pay for the same job as a white male. However, at the same time, the mantra is that "America can depend on Black women." They can be assured that Black women will overcome adversity with strength. Many Black women have grown up with the notion: "You are going to need to try twice as hard and be twice as good to succeed in America."

As a result, it is assumed that Black women do not need support. That they do not need encouragement. That they do not have the time to address their own trauma. That systemic disparities in employment, education, family responsibilities, health insurance, and other issues need not be addressed. That the expectations of Black women are warranted. The myth ensures that we are strong enough to endure yet another hardship, that we are not vulnerable.

The Strong Black Man

Research has confirmed what we already knew: Black men tend to be stereotyped as threatening and, as a result, are disproportionately targeted by police even when unarmed. Seven studies found that Black men are perceived as older, bigger, taller, heavier, more muscular, and stronger than white men, even when they are not. Thus, even small, slender Black males such as Tamir Rice (a twelve-year-old who looked younger), Trayvon Martin (a baby-faced seventeen-year-old), or Elijah McClain (a twenty-three-year-old, frail, glasses-wearing introvert) were not exempt from dying for being seen as strong, muscular, and intimidating (Wilson, Hugenberg, & Rule 2017). The race burden of the perceived strength of Black men is exacerbated by gender expectations:

> Based on gender alone, men have unique socialization experiences that encourage them to 'man up' (be courageous) and to

refrain from showing certain depression symptoms such as tearing up, displaying sad affect, or discussing feelings and emotions. Many men have specific concerns regarding masculinity (a desire to appear manly), so being seen as emotional is negative because it is considered a feminine trait. (Payne 2014, 80)

Black men are raised and socialized to refrain from expressing vulnerability and emotion. Partially as a self-protective mechanism, except for anger, they are less likely than women to convey emotion, self-disclose, or discuss pain or physical and mental distress experiences. Arthur Whaley coined the term "cultural distrust" to explain the guardedness and slowness to develop an alliance with a therapist (Whaley 2001). Based upon the threat that continues to exist against African American male lives, this reluctance to disclose is understandable. Black men are raised to "not be a punk" and to show a strong game face in all situations. African American males are taught to become hypervigilant about protecting their personal dignity, self-respect, and very lives (Williams 2000). Carrying that burden of invincibility, however, is taxing mentally, physically, and spiritually.

We (African Americans) are not strong; we are just human. And that is fine. We are not superheroes. It is okay to say that we need help at times. It is not decreasing our worth to step away from the myth and the hype regarding strength to endure. We have permission to exhale. We can heal our trauma as well. We, too, can allow ourselves to be pulled out of the fire.

ACT is unique because it uses metaphors and exercises to assist a person toward being more psychologically flexible. ACT helps a person learn how to move toward their values as they assess what truly "is" regarding their situations. Here is an exercise and metaphor to use with African Americans before getting into more in-depth acceptance work.

EXERCISE: Living as a Strong Black Person

A worksheet for this exercise is also available at http://www.newharbinger.com/49883.

Imagine that you are a strong Black person, as we have been taught to be. You may already consider yourself one! Sit in a chair. Relax and imagine that your lap is empty. As you relax there, imagine that I give you something to hold. Each time I give you something, imagine that each thing I give weighs a certain amount—like a barbell.

As I give you each of these things to hold, I am not giving you the option of saying no to receiving it. You must take it on because, after all, you are a strong Black woman or man. Each time I give you something, say out loud, "I am a strong Black woman!" or "I am a strong Black man!" One at a time, I give you these things to hold in your lap:

- Your present family and anyone in your household—ten pounds each

- Your relationship problems with any family or household member—ten more pounds per relationship problem

- Your finances—ten pounds

- Your struggle if you are not where you want to be financially—ten more pounds

- Your lack of social support, absence of good friends, and feelings of loneliness—ten pounds

- Your medical concerns and any health problems you may be having—twenty pounds each

- Your addictions to anything you are having difficulty stopping—twenty pounds each

- Your past losses, which still affect you—twenty pounds each

- Your traumatic experiences and any traumatic event that affected you—thirty pounds each

- Your experiences during COVID-19—thirty pounds

- Your experience of the effects of social unrest, racism, and discrimination—thirty pounds

- Your other burdens not mentioned—ten pounds each

Now sit for a moment with the accumulated weight of all that you are holding in your lap. Sit for a while and answer: How do you feel right now? What are your thoughts?

Finally, stand up from that chair and sit in another chair in the room. Imagine that you are a neutral observer, looking at your burdened self in the first chair, holding all that weight. What advice would you give to that strong Black person, sitting there with all that weight on them?

It Is What It Is

We pretend life is different than it is for so many reasons. I love the story "The Emperor's New Clothes," a childhood favorite by Hans Christian Andersen. I love it as a life lesson, and I have taught it more than once in my church. You likely know the story: An emperor loved new clothes so much that he spent all his money on being well-dressed. He cared nothing about training his soldiers, making sound judgments, or addressing townsfolk concerns, except to show off his new clothes.

One day, two swindlers came to town, who said they could weave the most magnificent fabrics imaginable with colors and patterns that were exceedingly beautiful. Also, clothes made of this cloth had a fantastic way of becoming invisible to anyone unfit for his career or who was unusually stupid. The whole town knew about the cloth's peculiar power, and all were impatient to find out how stupid their neighbors were.

Of course, the emperor had to have a coat made of that fabric. He paid the two swindlers a large sum of money to start work at once. They set up two looms and pretended to weave, though there was actually nothing on the looms. They worked the empty looms far into the night. Leaders and officers went to the room and couldn't see anything, but they didn't say so for fear of being declared stupid. They told the emperor, "Oh, it's beautiful—it's enchanting." "Such a pattern! What colors!" "Magnificent! What a design!"

The emperor didn't see anything either. His mind went through thoughts, as our minds sometimes do: "Am I a fool?" "Am I unfit for my office?" "Why did this happen to me?" So, the emperor covered up his inability to see too and instead declared, "Oh! It's so elegant, it has my highest approval."

So, the emperor put on the invisible clothes and had a procession throughout the town! Everyone in the streets and the windows said, "Oh, how fine are the emperor's new clothes! Don't they fit him to perfection? And see his long train!" Nobody would confess that they couldn't see anything, for that would prove them either unfit for their position or a fool.

"*But he hasn't got anything on*," a little child said.

From the time that we are little children, what happens to us that we begin to deny the truth about our lives as adults? Is it peer pressure? Is it fear of retribution? Or is it fear about really facing the ugly truth about something?

"It is what it is" can mean several things, depending on how it is said and the tone in which it is delivered. Basically, it means that it (whatever "it" is) is not going to change. "It" might not be the best scenario, but there is no wishing or hoping or dreaming for it to be different than it is. The phrase's connotation is that this is a less than favorable situation, but let's face this. Let's accept this reality. Let's deal with this. The phrase is used to remind us of the unalterable elements in life.

What this phrase does is help stop the struggle with negative situations or information. When my husband and I were experiencing challenges in our marriage, much of my struggle was in the expectation that maybe my marriage could be better if I just had a better attitude about it. Or maybe, even though it was not the best now, it had the *potential* to be good. Or… taking account of all the investment of years of time and energy I made into this relationship, it *should* be better than it is. Or, maybe it wasn't better because of some character flaw I have. Perhaps it's my fault and responsibility, and if so, possibly I have the power to make it better.

Look. It is what it is. Face it.

The movement toward getting emotionally unstuck includes awareness and truthful acceptance of where we are in our pain. In the next chapter, we will discuss how selectively letting go can move us closer to personal and emotional freedom.

CHAPTER 4

"Freedom to Let Go"— Cognitive Defusion

All the time and energy that you waste on struggling with thoughts and feelings could be far more usefully invested in taking effective action...Thoughts are merely words, symbols, or bits of language, so why declare war on them?

—Russ Harris, *The Happiness Trap*

I was twenty-six years old when my father died. I remember it so clearly. At the time, I worked full-time as a medical caseworker. My father had been hospitalized several times over the past two years, staying overnight or a few days at a time. I knew that my father had been in the hospital this time for about a week, but I had not visited him.

My father was a great father when it came to his role as the provider and protector of the home. He was a supervisor with the US Postal Service and well-liked at his job. He had always provided for his family, buying cars for my mother and me when I came of age. Yet, my father was always emotionally distant. I know now it was because he had never learned how to express emotion. Still, while I was growing up, it was excruciating, especially in my teenage years.

I do not recall him ever telling me that he loved me, and I wanted that approval desperately as time went by. I felt like if I was able to please him, he would love me. I remember once that I had a great report card, all As and one B+. He looked at the report card and immediately asked, "Why isn't this grade an A?" The theme "I'm not enough" developed in my teenage years from my interactions with my father and others. By the time I completed high school, I had become resentful that my father could never express love for me as I was. So, I began to emotionally draw away from him.

My father never talked about any pain that he may have been going through. This made sense; he was a World War II veteran and had likely suffered various traumatic experiences in childhood. Although he never discussed them, it was known that he left home earlier than age eighteen for some reason. As I matured, I began to understand his hard, staunch exterior. But in my early years, his demeanor was too painful for me to understand. My father was always so big in my eyes, bigger than life. He was almost like a superhero. As a child, I would look up to see his face, and he seemed invincible. The fact that he never talked about his pain—not to me, not to my mother, not to anyone—just strengthened my thought that he was Superman.

So, when my father was in the hospital again this particular time, I hadn't even gone to visit him. I was still resentful. I was still angry. And part of me thought that he would come out of the hospital again like he did last time. If he did not want to talk to his family about what was going on with him (he never disclosed), then who was I to try to beat it out of him.

I was sitting at my desk in the late morning, trying to work. Still, something kept pressing upon me to get up, ask my supervisor if I could leave for the day, and go to the hospital to see my father. The conviction to leave was spiritually heavy over me, like a cloak, so I followed it. And when I went to the hospital and went into my father's room, I immediately knew that something was dreadfully wrong with my father. This man before me was not the big, looming, strong man that I knew. This was a man on a ventilator with several tubes, a small and shrunken man who only slightly resembled my father. I knew in my heart that he was near death as soon as I saw him.

I can remember that day like it was yesterday. I went to his bed and immediately said that I was so sorry that I had not come to visit him until now. I cried by his bedside. My father couldn't speak—whatever ailed him had taken his ability to talk. There was a glass of water with a straw near his bedside. I asked him if I could help him drink, and his eyes said yes. Again, this is something that this big strong man would never do—allow me to help him as he was in a weak position. I cried some more. I knew that his eyes told me that he loved me, even if he couldn't say the words. And on that very same day, within an hour of my visit, my father yielded and died.

Even now, as I write this so many years later, fresh tears fall from my eyes. Mainly because I am so very grateful that I had that last moment with my father. I am so thankful that I listened to God's strong urging and went to see him. And I am so glad that my father was able to hold onto life until I came to see him.

But I tell that story to discuss what happened after my father died. After my father died, no one else asked, "Why didn't you get an A instead of an A- or a B"? There was no one else expecting me to achieve greatness with every report card or with every endeavor. But I was surprised and shocked to find out that, although my father died, that voice continued to speak to me. "You are not enough." in my late twenties, in my thirties, and beyond. "You need to do more." "That's not good enough." "Why didn't you do better?" "You have to do better than that" "You don't belong in this master's program." "You don't belong in this doctoral PhD program." "You don't belong in this job." That voice... Those old tapes continued to play...and play...and play. I thought that when my father was buried, those old tapes would be buried along with him. But they remained alive. Why were they still alive? Why wouldn't they shut up?

Those old tape recordings (MP3s or DVDs for those too young to remember tapes) plagued me. They influenced my academic endeavors. I always felt that I needed to do more—achieve more, be more organized, and have more impact. They influenced my romantic relationships because I thought (in the past, not now) that I did not deserve a good man in my life. So, I found myself gravitating towards and dating who I thought were "underdogs." Those who I thought deserved a chance in life and love. I did not look for relationship partners; I looked for relationship projects because I had that thought that I was "not good enough." These old tapes influenced everything in my life.

The old tapes also influenced my emotions. I was always living in a chronic state of anxiety, feeling like a ball would drop somewhere. When I was in undergraduate courses at UCLA, one of my favorite cartoons at the time was Ziggy. Ziggy was a character who always thought the worst was going to happen to him. Even when fortune happened, Ziggy believed that Murphy's Law would take place and something was going to mess it up. I thought Ziggy was funny because I identified with Ziggy. I even called myself "Ziggy" as a nickname and asked others to call me that as well. Those old tapes got me identifying with a cartoon character with a big, round, fat head who was always depressed.

I cannot describe the constant state of anxiety that I lived in, but I can say that it was highly uncomfortable. It was painful. It hurt a great deal. It had my stomach tied up in knots and kept me from truly experiencing pleasure. Those thoughts—the self-limiting beliefs, the harsh self-criticisms—had taken on a life of their own, and I began to believe them more than the sound of my own voice. Listening to those thoughts started to influence my behavior. I would not attempt to connect to other classmates because I already thought they felt I didn't belong. I would not allow anyone to get too close to me for fear that they would find out my secret: I was a fraud.

If you have old tapes playing in your head too, the anxiety may be making you tired all the time like I was. I was constantly in my own head, hearing the thoughts, then trying to fight them or control them. Trying to manipulate them, avoid them, shut them out, or eliminate them. Trying to wrestle with them and conquer them. Tensing my body and gritting my teeth against the wave of them, resenting them. I was exhausted all the time, tuckered out from unsuccessful attempts at control.

I will tell you a secret. Even to this day, there are times when these same old tapes play in my mind. The purpose of ACT is not to get rid of your thoughts. It is not to banish thoughts and magically make your life rosier and your emotions permanently joyful. But what I can say is that these thoughts won't have power over you like they had before. If and when these old tapes play (which will be less often), you will see their messages more like a stranger in the distance than an all-powerful thought. That is the beauty of ACT. You can learn to let go of the struggle with unpleasant thoughts. And you can begin to live a life where you are doing what matters most to you, without those old tapes getting in the way.

Cultural Influences on Those Old Tapes

Some of us who are Black were brought up with specific cultural thoughts and notions. If we allowed them, these cultural notions could paralyze us or slow our progress toward our own values. As I look at my tapes, I realize that there was also a cultural influence on why and how these tapes developed the way they did. My father meant well; he did not mean me harm by trying to instill in me a desire to take education seriously. I understood his and my mother's background. As African Americans born in the early part of the 1900s, they both had experiences that shaped how they functioned. They shared their own experiences of racism growing up. My mom had to work as a maid because there were no opportunities for Negroes (the word used back then) and she was treated horribly. My father did not talk to me about his experiences. However, I know that he suffered both in the war and after. He could not get educated during his day and time. So, he became adamant that his daughter should and would get educated. She would have a better life than he had, and education was the path to success and respect for African Americans. I was raised in a home where this mantra was said to me weekly: "Education is one thing that people can't take away from you. Education is one thing that will set you apart as a person with Black skin." I understand why he pushed me so hard. It was cultural.

Along with that cultural push toward education came other old tapes that are culturally based. You probably recognize these:

- "You know a Black person has to work more than twice as hard just to be recognized in the same position as a white person would."

- "You know they expect us to be lazy, so we have to prove them wrong."

- "You don't have time for crying, pouting, or all of that emotional stuff. That's a luxury only white people can afford. Girl, you better keep on pressing."

- "You better learn how to be a shape-shifter and a code-switcher. Act how you are expected to *act* in those outside spaces, so you can survive."

- "It doesn't matter how hard I work. They are only going to see my Blackness."

- "White people will always see me as a suspect. Hell, maybe I am suspect."

Whether the tapes were created (1) through a loved one speaking them to you, (2) via the culture in which you were raised, (3) from discriminatory experiences (Broman et al. 2000), or (4) you created them yourself, the origin story does not matter. In the end, it doesn't matter how these old tapes are produced. It does not matter if those thoughts are false, partially true, or 100 percent true. In the end, what matters is that you have old tapes (or Blu-rays or MP3s) playing in your head, getting in your own way, keeping you from your own values. What are they saying to you?

Handcuffs for Your Mind

I find it interesting that many of us Blacks think very clearly and negatively about somebody trying to trick, dupe, or swindle us. We will quickly kick someone out of our life who does this without a bat of an eyelash. If we think someone is trying to scam us, we will not only kick them to the curb but we will also quickly blast them and expose them in any way we can. I can speak for myself: I know for sure that if a business is attempting to swindle me, I would be on the Better Business Bureau website as fast as lightning. I would be exposing that business for what it is. Many of us will quickly create Instagram or Facebook posts to reveal that trickster. Many of us would quickly get hundreds of our followers to agree with us about how shady or wrong that business or person was. My pastor had a saying: "Don't pee on my back and tell me I'm sweating." As African Americans, we collectively have experienced adverse events in this country for over four hundred years. So, understandably, we might be particularly sensitive or resistant to getting tricked, duped, or swindled. That makes sense to me.

Yet, when those old tapes begin to play in our heads, why don't we have the same reaction as we would to a person or organization external to us? Why do we take those thoughts as if they were the Bible? "You are boring." "You are too stupid." "That's because you are ugly." "You will never get that." "You don't deserve a good relationship like that." And we sit there listening. Why is that?

ACT calls this "fusion" with our thoughts: "We begin to relate to the content of our mind as if it were a physical thing" (Bennett & Oliver, 48). I think of fusion as buying into the hype that is being said. What I mean is that many of us buy into what our thoughts are saying about us. Fusion, to me, is believing those old tapes that play as if they are gospel or came straight from God's mouth. We are handcuffed to these thoughts.

I think about handcuffs and what they symbolize to the Black community. Definitely, handcuffs have a negative connotation. When I think about handcuffs today, I think about the high levels of incarceration of Blacks in the United States. The Bureau of Justice Statistics reports extreme inequities by race regarding those imprisoned (Carson 2020). For every 100,000 Black residents in the United States, 1,096 are prisoners. This is compared with 525 Hispanic prisoners for every 100,000 Hispanic residents and 214 white prisoners for every 100,000 white residents (Carson 2020). This number does not address the level of illegal activity in a population. Some would like to believe that Blacks are imprisoned more because Blacks are more guilty of crimes than whites. But instead, it appears that the darker one's skin tone is, the more likely it is that a person might be imprisoned. Imprisoned rather than being given bail, probation, and a second chance at life. When reflecting on the thousands of Blacks who have been racially profiled over the years, we see this clearly. That racial profiling has resulted in so many lives being snatched by police even before they could stand before a judge in court.

The relationship between handcuffs and the African American community has always been tenuous. From the time our ancestors were brought to the United States in 1619, we were chained, shackled, and handcuffed. A little over four hundred years ago, our ancestors arrived in Virginia on a ship that bore us as human cargo. Those first Africans were kidnapped from their villages in present-day Angola. (This hit me hard when I learned it because I visited AfricanAncestry.com to check my DNA on my father's side and found that my family's bloodline is directly from Angola). Half of those 350 Africans who boarded that ship died before they reached land (Shipp 2019). Onboard, the Africans were stripped of all of their clothes, thoroughly and roughly examined, packed together, and secured by leg irons and shackles. They were exposed to violence, sexual abuse from the crew, lack of sanitation, and suffocating conditions. They were force-fed like cattle. This was just the beginning of the four-hundred-plus-year relationship with handcuffs, shackles, and captivity.

I think about all of the men and women subjected to chains, hand-cuffs, and shackles over the years, from the time the first ships landed until well past the Emancipation Proclamation. I think about how Martin Luther King Jr. was handcuffed several times (Rothman 2015). Two examples were in (1) 1956 when he was arrested during the Montgomery bus boycott and (2) in 1960 when he wore handcuffs for refusing to leave his seat at a segregated Atlanta department store lunch counter. I think of the Blacks who have been jailed or handcuffed over the past few centuries in America. And I think about the racial profiling that continues today. I think about George Floyd and how he was handcuffed with a knee on his neck until he died. I think of the collective intergenerational and historical trauma that has taken place over the years and how handcuffs have been a symbol of captivity for us as a people. The point I am attempting to make is that handcuffs mean a great deal to Blacks in America.

Let's think about handcuffs for a moment. Handcuffs are specially made items that are designed to restrain people's ability to move their upper bodies. They are usually made with metal or some other hard substance. They are made to slide onto people's wrists, and they typically are linked together by a chain, a hinge, or a rigid bar. Once they're on a person's wrists, they cannot be pulled off or opened. Without the key to that particular set of handcuffs, one cannot open them. And a curious thing about handcuffs is that the more you move, wriggle, or try to slide out of them, the tighter they will clamp on your wrist. Handcuffs are made to tighten as you resist, until they are incredibly uncomfortable.

Because handcuffs are such a powerful symbol for us, I describe fusion as "handcuffs on your mind." Let's use the idea "I'm not enough" that I learned as a child as an example. Even though those are just words, they took on a life of their own in my childhood. Those three words:

- became my reason to refrain from trying new things

- gave me knots in my stomach and nightmares at night

- began to influence how I lived life and if I decided to engage in activities that I valued

- moved from being inanimate objects to being handcuffs and shackles on my mind.

This is how your fusion works too. There are four types of fusion with thoughts (Bennett & Oliver 2019). Those types of fusion can be reframed in this way:

Handcuffed to worries or thoughts about future	Handcuffed to thoughts about the past
Handcuffed to thoughts about yourself or other people	Handcuffed to rules and "should have" or "could have"

When I think about us accepting those negative thoughts and old tapes as if they were living, breathing entities that have the power to hold us down, I get sad. I think about the term "learned helplessness" in psychology.

Fused to Helplessness

Martin Seligman first did experiments on the learned helplessness phenomenon in dogs. After the dogs were shocked with electricity enough times, they would not try to get out of the area where they were shocked, even if there was a clear opening for them to get out. As African Americans who have experienced institutional and isolated discrimination in our lives, some have also developed a learned helplessness mentality.

I can remember, many years ago, when I was in a bad financial situation. I had two very young daughters and a husband who was not financially supportive. In addition, I was attempting to get more education—I was in a master's program at the time. I wanted and needed to do everything legal and moral that I could to keep my babies fed and well-cared-for while I was in school. I was fortunate to obtain a few scholarships. Still, I also needed to go on welfare temporarily so that my children and I would have medical coverage and the basic necessities.

I will always recall what it was like sitting in those Department of Public Social Service waiting rooms. At that time, even if one had an appointment, often someone could sit in the waiting room for hours before being called. I remember sitting there and looking at some of the other mothers in the room. The look on many of their faces was quiet resignation. As a social worker in training, I found it terrible that these mothers had to sit for hours in a crowded space just to get help. There was also a mandate back then that moms had to bring their young child to the office. Eligibility workers needed to physically see the child to prove that mothers were not lying about having a child. There was a mother across from me whose baby was one week old. That mother sat there for hours, with her one-week-old child in her arms, quietly waiting to be called. Few people asked when they were going to be seen. It was as if this treatment was expected and was considered normal.

This, to me, is what learned helplessness looks like. This is what it looks like when the fight is completely knocked out of a person or a people. When some people become resigned to the state they are in, they do not try to get out of that negative situation because the past has taught them that they are helpless—there is no way out. Years and generations of ill-treatment taught these mothers that it was just a part of life for them to wait hours for help. It taught them that their need for financial assistance was shameful and that waiting was warranted. We will talk more about how to move out of learned helplessness in chapter eight.

Fusion, then, is believing the hype that is in our own heads about ourselves. For me, although my father was long gone and buried, my thoughts continued to keep me captive and kept me from what I truly desired for my life. Fusion is a prison of our own making. The sad thing is that, even after the prison door is opened, some of us remain in that prison cell, paralyzed in a corner. Some of us are just surviving, not thriving. And some of us feel that we don't deserve to thrive and live our values; we have been so beaten down by life. But there is a way out of being fused to our own thoughts. There is a way out.

Defusing Your Mind

How can a particular thought obtain life in and of itself? How can that thought become larger than life? How can it become big, large and in charge, and highly time-consuming? How can it start calling the shots, and how can we bow down to it and serve it, living our lives under its shadow? It is a type of prison—a thought prison.

ACT helps us to alter our relationship with thoughts, freeing us from an enslaver/enslaved person relationship with each thought. It helps us to stop limiting ourselves or keeping ourselves in a box. ACT can move us from being reactive to proactive. It can move us away from being so focused on our thoughts that we are putting out fires. Because we are not getting anything meaningful to us accomplished.

ACT is not a magic wand; it will not eliminate the thoughts for us, and it will not stop the thoughts from being painful. However, we can learn how to stop being tossed to-and-fro by the thoughts like a ragdoll.

We can learn how to stop getting beat up by thoughts. We can unshackle ourselves from those thoughts. ACT does not eliminate the fire of those thoughts, but it can take the shackles off our feet so we can dance in the fire. ACT can give us the freedom to let go of the prison of words that we sometimes dwell in. We can obtain a healthy distance from our thoughts. This is the defusion process. As Steven C. Hayes writes in the book *Get Out of Your Mind and Into Your Life*, "What we need to learn to do is to look at thought, rather than from thought."

Story: *Fused to Harmful Habits*

Maya is a thirty-three-year-old Black woman who was asked by her physician to speak with her nurse to discuss a plan to get her diabetes and her weight under control. Maya is over seventy-five pounds overweight and she has an A1C of 7.5 (diabetic levels). Her nurse talked with her to discuss behavior change, to avoid the need for insulin shots.

Maya explained to her nurse that she has been overweight her whole life. "Even when I was a baby, my mom told me that I was the greediest of her three children. She said I used to lick the plate clean when I was a toddler." When asked if they could formulate a plan together about how to address her eating and exercise habits, she said, "I'm a fatty. I have always been a fatty, and I will probably always be a fatty. What's the use in trying? I probably have tried everything there is to lose weight."

When her nurse asked her what she eats in a typical day, she answered, "I know, I know. I'm supposed to be eating brussels sprouts and green beans. I'm supposed to be eating artichokes and cauliflower. But I hate that stuff. I know what I'm supposed to be doing, believe me. I've heard it over and over."

Her nurse talked with her about the possibility of having to go on insulin instead of pills soon, and she said, "Well, I'm not surprised. Both my parents had type 2 diabetes, and some of my other relatives. I guess I'm destined to have a future where I lose my eyesight and maybe lose a foot to diabetes."

As Maya had this discussion with her nurse, she looked sad. Her eyes were cast down, and she looked at the point of tears. If Maya had expressed her feelings during that discussion, she would have said, "I'm depressed, ashamed, embarrassed, defeated, angry at myself, fearful, and worried about my future."

Maya's thoughts have her stuck in harmful habits. If she is to better her health without insulin, she must face the thoughts. If Maya had decided to go to a therapist who uses cognitive behavioral therapy, she would have probably been taught to logically challenge her thoughts. Maya's therapist might have asked her about the truthfulness of her thoughts about herself and the world.

But if Maya had instead decided to go to an ACT therapist, she would not experience having someone try to logically challenge her thoughts or feelings. Instead, an ACT therapist would help her to find out if she was shackled or handcuffed to the thoughts she expressed or not. Some questions an ACT therapist might ask include:

- Maya, are you able to notice when thoughts are doing you wrong or taking you down a path you don't want to go down?

- Is the thought "I'll always be a fatty" keeping you hostage or as a prisoner?

- Are your thoughts about your weight stunting your growth toward your own values?

- How is that thought "I'll always be a fatty" working for you?

- Maya, are we able to "unhook" from these thoughts? Can we get the shackles of this thought off so that you can move toward what matters to you?

Maya may have told an ACT therapist that she actually valued good health, despite her thoughts and beliefs about herself. She did want to have a long life where she was not suffering from the problems associated with diabetes. So, an ACT therapist would have helped Maya to develop the skills needed to *defuse*: to unlock the handcuffs and unshackle herself from thoughts she was having so that she can move toward her value of good health.

Freedom to Let Go

For African Americans, the concept of freedom is everything. It is a collective value that we are unified in ascribing to, mainly because of our history of having a lack of it in the United States. Because of that, control is a significant issue, especially for those who feel they have no control. As we discussed in the last chapter, when we cannot control some things in life (like the racial climate in this country and how it affects us), we sometimes try to control those things that we think are within our control. So, we believe that we should be able to control our thoughts. They are *our* thoughts, after all. Since we perceive little control over some outside factors, we may think, "I can control what goes in and out of my body. I can control my own thought processes."

The problem with attempting to control is that we try to reign over certain things, like our thoughts. We manipulate and try to avoid specific thoughts, or we attempt to distract ourselves from certain things. We do all kinds of things to attain control because, again, at least we should have control over these things. But the problem is when we try to lock down and control our thoughts in any way, those thoughts are locking us down as well.

Call to mind one of your tapes, a thought you are fused to. Are you holding onto that thought tightly? At the same time that you are holding onto something tightly, that same thing is clamped onto you tightly. Many of us have had the experience of wearing real or toy handcuffs. I used to have play handcuffs. The handcuff was tight around my wrist. When I struggled, it just got tighter. The more I wrestled, the more uncomfortable things got. It became tight and constrictive. The only way to get out of the handcuffs was to calmly use a key. And when the handcuffs were off, they did not hold any menace. They were not scary or painful. Just a piece of metal. Same thing with the shackles our ancestors used to wear when they were enslaved. There was no way to claim victory over the handcuffs or shackles as long as they were on our bodies and we were wrestling with them. We needed to calmly find a key to unlock them.

EXERCISE: Handcuffs on the Table

A worksheet for this exercise is also available at http://www.newharbinger.com/49883.

Imagine that there is a table before you. Now imagine that there is a pair of handcuffs on the table. Look, in your mind, at the handcuffs. Imagine the texture of the handcuffs, how they might feel if you merely put a finger on them and touched them. Are they cold? Imagine what they are made of. See in your mind's eye the color of them. Imagine how much they might weigh. All of this while the handcuffs are still sitting on the table.

The handcuffs have never moved. They are sitting on top of the table. They cannot move without someone picking them up. How much power do the handcuffs have now as they sit on the table? How important are they when they are not being used? Think for a moment about the handcuffs being on the table and how powerless they are. Without being used, they are simply two circles of metal tied together. Breathe in a deep breath and breathe out, still looking at the handcuffs on the table in your mind's eye.

Now think about one of the thoughts that trip you up and keep you from doing things that really matter to you. Choose just one thought. What thought did you choose?

Okay, imagine that one thought and see it as handcuffs. You could see it any way you want. Maybe you see the words themselves formed into two circles with a line in the middle. Or, perhaps you imagine each word making up your thought engraved on the handcuffs on the table. Whichever way you see it, see that thought as handcuffs.

And now, in your mind's eye, place those word handcuffs onto your wrists. You can put your wrists out before you now, as you sit in your chair, and imagine that the words that make up your thought are tied around your wrists like handcuffs. There is no way out of the handcuffs by simply wrestling with them. Instead, imagine the handcuffs tightening if you try to avoid the thought or wrestle with it.

Sit for a moment with the weight of those word handcuffs binding you. How do you feel now? What are you thinking?

Finally, get up from your chair and sit in a chair next to the first one. Imagine that you are a neutral observer, looking at yourself in the first chair with those words handcuffing your wrists. What advice would you give to that person in the first chair who is shackled to those words?

Here are the big questions that we can always ask ourselves to assess whether we are in captivity or if we are walking in freedom based on a thought (Harris 2019):

Is what you're doing working to give you the sort of life you want, in the long term?

How is that (behavior, thought, feeling) working for you?

Are you tightly holding onto that thought? Then that thought is also holding you. You can learn the skill, the key, to let go and attain freedom. Then that thought, like a pair of handcuffs sitting on a table, has no power whatsoever. There is hope for us to unhook ourselves from the thoughts and feelings that bind us and keep us stuck. The next chapter is "In the Here and Now"—Present Moment Awareness. In it, we will discuss how to escape being stuck in the past or paralyzed worrying about the future.

CHAPTER 5

"In the Here and Now"— Present Moment Awareness

If you must look back, do so forgivingly. If you must look forward, do so prayerfully. However, the wisest thing you can do is to be present in the present. Gratefully.

—Maya Angelou

Marcel had a disability that made him unable to walk well. He had over twenty-five surgeries during his lifetime to treat complications of his disability. None of the surgeries were able to fully repair his mobility or condition. In addition, Marcel had a very challenging and traumatic childhood due to his disabilities, family problems, and economic struggles. As he got older, his chronic illnesses became more complex and affected his life more and more. He began experiencing pain more often than before—both physical and emotional.

To deal with his ongoing emotional and physical pain related to the disability, Marcel reframed parts of his childhood and youth. He thought less often about his childhood and adulthood, and more often about his high school days when he felt he was his best self. At age fifty, Marcel would talk a great deal about his high school successes. He loved to discuss how popular he was in high school and what his life was like then. He also talked a great deal about his experiences in his twenties—his job successes back then, his ease with friendships and relationships. Marcel idealized his relationships during high school and saw his twenties as golden years in his life.

He focused on this glamorized time of his life almost every day. He talked with a high school friend every week about how things were back then in high school for them and began to use that time of his life to define himself. Yet, the life he lived in the present, in his fifties, became more and more incongruent with the life he talked about back then. He sat in a chair from day to day, either watching TV to distract himself or talking on the telephone about his past to a family member or old friend. He did not move toward any particular personal value or goal.

And sadly, Marcel began to waste away in his La-Z-Boy chair, moving from cane to walker to wheelchair. He denied that he was actually aging. The aging process in all of us causes us to adjust our lifestyles, but he denied that his disability may need particular actions or additional adjustments as he aged. So, he got physically worse. He was caught in a cycle; focused so much on the past that he ignored the present and future.

In addition to what was said about Marcel, it is important to note that he was a Black male, experiencing all that comes along with being a Black male in America. Thus, no one knows how many acts of discrimination Marcel suffered based on the combination of race or ability, and how those acts affected his self-esteem. Marcel died from medical complications that might have been potentially delayed or stopped if he had faced his present-day pain.

Sadly, some of us may have a similar story. We may not have a physical disability but instead an emotional, situational, or mental hindrance. Regardless of what type of hindrance they have, some people tragically die in paralysis and inaction, never moving toward their own values.

Stuck in the Past: Keeping It Moving

Living in the present can be extremely hard for everyone. African Americans, though, have additional factors that can make it difficult. Sometimes, people live in the past, like Marcel did, because they idealized some small spot of their life that felt comfortable to them. Other times, people live in the past because their pasts have never been addressed. Maybe they tried to sweep them under the rug, but they keep coming back up in their present lives like vomit because they were never addressed.

I said this in a previous chapter, but I will repeat this. Black people endured four-hundred-plus years of a negative experience in America, yet that experience has never been adequately addressed. Not in interventions, not through acknowledgments even.

Another reason why it is so hard to live in the present for African Americans is that painful events continue to happen. Along with those past unaddressed historical traumas, hurts, and pains, continual present hurts keep coming. Continued racial slights. Continual microaggressions. Continual killings through racial profiling.

I have experienced many racial slights—I clearly recall one in particular that I experienced in the not-too-distant past. I was at a professional conference, talking in the conference lobby with a white female colleague when a white male approached us. The man, there for reasons other than the conference, was checking out of the hotel. My colleague and I were standing nowhere near the checkout desk. Also, I was dressed professionally and deep in conversation with someone. Despite these things, this man proceeded to interrupt our conversation and say to me, "You can take my bags to my car now."

To be honest, I do not exactly remember what I said to the man in response. I remember the event as if it were happening in slow motion. I saw the surprised look on my colleague's face, and I also noticed what she did not do. The white woman colleague who was with me said nothing to the man. She did not correct him but just stood there. I do not recall what I said to the man in response, but I know I said something polite. A polite set of words redirecting the man in a polite tone. All types of emotions flooded me at that moment, but the thought that prevailed was, "What if I become the angry Black woman that he expects?" So, instead of addressing him, I reacted automatically, pretending that I did not understand that his racial slight was a racial slight.

Black people can experience minimizations and racial slights just like that—at the snap of a finger. So, how does present awareness work for someone who never had the chance to deal with a past hurt? And how does present awareness work for a culture that teaches that you need to keep it moving despite what has happened to you?

A hurt, a sore, an emotional pain occurred in your life. Someone might not have protected you from harm when you were a child. Someone might have engaged in an unthinkable or evil act against you in your childhood or adulthood. Someone might have disappointed you and not lived up to their promises to you, or they might have used you or taken advantage of you. Someone might have said or done something harmful to your child or your loved ones. You might have gone through and suffered a major loss in an area. People close to you might have died or become ill and dependent on you. You might have been bullied or talked about, defrauded, or stolen from. You might have suffered traumatic events in your life. But you got up and kept it moving.

You may have just pushed what happened in your background, in your subconscious, and it still affects you today. It affects you because you have problems sleeping at night. It affects you because of the nightmares you have. It affects you because sometimes, overwhelming anxiety or sadness catches you off guard. It affects you because what you did was you put a Band-Aid on it and pretended it was okay. It affects your outlook on life because you might "keep it moving," all the while still feeling like the world is dangerous, scary, and unpredictable. Or thinking that people will hurt you and cannot be trusted. You say you are okay, yet you judge your new relationships by what happened to you in your old ones. This is baggage, even though you don't think you have it.

But it is still affecting you! If it wasn't, you wouldn't be doing what is called the *repetition compulsion*. The repetition compulsion is defined in psychology as some people's propensity to repeatedly reenact early life experiences, even if they do not want to. To engage in the same self-defeating thoughts and behaviors over and over.

It takes courage to face your need for healing. It takes courage to admit to yourself that you have not been functioning whole. It takes courage to not only live life in the present but to also potentially re-open a past wound that was just Band-aided. Some injuries should not have just had a quick Band-Aid placed over them. Some wounds need to be re-opened or at least faced so that the pus of bitterness, regret, unforgiveness, self-blame, and shame can be lanced out. Some injuries are infected and need to be addressed and cleaned before they can be healed.

So, how can you separate things to stay aware of in the present from things you should deal with from the past? How can you address present moment awareness while at the same time acknowledging and addressing past issues that have not been dealt with? These are questions we will explore further, later in the chapter.

Time Hopping and Living in the Future

All humans have the potential to suffer from worry about the future. Often, though, our fear about the future stems from a past or present negative experience. For example, I wonder how many people are worried about their livelihood and financial well-being after experiencing a global pandemic. Some are afraid that they may not continue working or paying for their necessities, based on the past and present experiences that they had during COVID-19.

You may not be able to stop your mind from racing forward to fixate on what could potentially go wrong. You could have a hard time keeping your mind from drifting ahead to what could happen in the future, bad or good. And when you live trying to second guess the future, forecast and predict the future, or somehow control or shape the future, you are often living in a frenzied, anxiety-filled state. It is definitely not a peaceful state of existence, looking and constantly straining toward the future, trying to avoid a pain that has not yet arrived.

As I wrote this book, I strived to be transparent and share authentically. I am saying this now because I am about to share a vulnerable moment. When I look back at my childhood, I was a very anxious child. I was overly concerned with planning, calendars, looking ahead, datebooks, and schedules, even at a young age. When I was twelve, I was thinking about what thirteen would be like. And when I was thirteen, I was desperately trying to rush away painful thirteen to better days. I was always anxious or concerned about things. I was worried that I was not doing enough to get the grades I needed so that Daddy would tell me, "Good job." I was afraid that I was not being social enough in junior high to be liked in high school. I was concerned that I was not skinny enough, or tall enough, or outgoing enough. I imagined myself becoming something that I was not yet—a polished, sophisticated, intelligent, thin, beautiful scientist. Maybe a neurophysicist, or perhaps a microbiologist, neither of which I knew anything about. I longed to see myself as what I was not. I certainly did not want to see myself at the weight I was, with the clothes I had on, with the hairstyle I had, with the personality I had at the time.

I wonder how much of my anxiety at not being who I was at the time was influenced by messages I heard over the years about being Black. Messages about beauty, how beauty was not brown skin, how beauty was not kinky hair, or how beauty was not a certain weight or build. My desire to be anything than what I was in junior high was affected by many things, including society's views of what it meant to be Black in America.

I remember, well into my twenties and thirties, how I would live my life from epiphany to epiphany, from big task to the next. I would live for graduation day, or I would live for my wedding day, or I would live for the day my baby was born. I would live for the significant events in life, but I would not enjoy the process of living along the way. I'd run from task to task, without experiencing the journey. But when we get too far ahead of ourselves, we drive ourselves crazy. We aren't living in the moment or experiencing our actual present circumstances. We are just surviving until the next big thing.

Also, future versus present moment thinking is exacerbated by the times we live in. As African Americans, if we don't feel safe or think it might be our loved ones on the news being racially profiled or killed (or us), then we live in anticipation of what negative things might happen. And since this is a real threat, it is difficult to handle. Of course, being informed is crucial and has many essential benefits. However, there is a lot of information through technology coming at us that can multiply our worries. Think of all of the scary and devastating headlines in our newsfeed, the frightening news from friends and loved ones. These days, most of us have a first-hand heightened awareness about what could go wrong.

Story: *No Comfort in the Past or Future*

Andre is a thirty-year-old Black male who has been experiencing severe depression and anxiety. Although he is not suicidal, he feels like life does not matter. His wife, Tina, with whom he has been in a relationship since high school, is very concerned about him.

Andre's behavior change started a little bit before COVID-19 began to affect the world. At that time, Andre was working as an assistant manager at a sporting goods store. As he was driving home after work one evening, he got pulled over by the police because one of his back taillights was out. One of the two officers who pulled him over harassed him. The officer drew his gun on Andre, forcefully telling him to get out of the car. He had Andre sit on the curb while the officer illegally searched his vehicle and his trunk. When the officer found nothing of importance, he appeared to get more agitated.

Andre did everything that his family taught him to do. He spoke calmly. He did not raise his arms or his voice; he moved slowly. However, the officer continued to get more agitated and began to accuse Andre of acts he had not done. The second officer remained quiet and did nothing for most of this encounter. As the first officer became increasingly angry, the second one finally convinced the first officer to leave the scene after giving Andre a ticket for the broken taillight.

Not long after this incident, Andre witnessed, along with the world, the video of the George Floyd murder. While he was attempting to process this, he was laid off from his job due to COVID. Thus, Andre had more time on his hands at home, and he had more time to think about how he was George Floyd, and George Floyd was him.

To distract himself, Andre began to become obsessed with certain types of social media. In particular, he began to follow social media personalities that promoted nihilism—the belief in nothing, life has no meaning, and political and social institutions have no purpose. He developed deep cultural distrust against "the establishment." He would talk to his wife and his eight-year-old son, Andre Jr., about his belief that there is nothing to be trusted in America. The legal system, political system, and the whole way *things are set up are corrupt. He also distrusted doctors, researchers, and the news media. He became adamant about not taking the COVID-19 immunizations because there was something sinister behind the whole way COVID-19 and the immunizations came about. He listened fervently to those who forecasted and predicted significant catastrophic events that they said would take place this year in this country. And he felt that he could never go back to "life as usual," where he was a pawn and servant working to put more money into the pockets of the rich and people who did not look like him.*

Andre was convinced of a horrible future and despaired about changing or avoiding a doomsday that was undoubtedly coming. He began to lose a significant amount of weight, and he could not sleep; he would pace in the kitchen most nights while others were asleep. He became indifferent to doing things with the family such as outings or playing catch with his son like he used to do. He stopped making efforts to look for another job, and he was often irritable. He would snap at his wife or son with little provocation.

"I just want the Andre back that we love," Tina would say.

In the Here and Now

The problem with being stuck in the past or predicting the future is that neither is real. The past and future are only in our minds because our feet are planted solidly in the right here/right now. No amount of wishing or dreaming the "right now" away will change it from being what it is. In reality, all we can manipulate is this space and time that we are now in.

So, what does it mean to be present? Being present is being able to notice your "here and now." It is the ability to detect the "now" about your life without panic or anxiety. Instead, we can learn to be aware of the here and now in a curious, open way. Whether things are great for you right now or not as you would like, present moment awareness is a skill that enables you to notice and think about your new experience. Why is this important? Because the only movement that you can make toward what really matters to you occurs in the here and now, not in the past or future (Harris 2019).

Another reason why being present is important is because being stuck focused on the past or trying to forecast the future takes extreme mental energy that actually solves nothing. This mental energy drain can eventually exhaust you and leave you depleted, depressed, anxious, or joyless. Being a Black person in America is tiring enough, without adding insult to injury by focusing on the past or future. Pastor John R. Faison Sr., a senior pastor of Watson Grove Baptist Church in Nashville, said it well in his article "A Letter to White People: Black Americans Are Exhausted" (Faison Sr. 2020). In the article, Pastor Faison talks about his exhaustion as a Black man in America. He explains the multiple weights that are pressing upon every part of who we are as Black Americans. He eloquently states:

> My body is exhausted. The emotional and psychological weights of this season are having a physical toll. My body feels the continual tension of having to fight two viruses: COVID-19 and COVID-1619…The tension in my shoulders. The unconscious clenching of my jaw. The knots in my stomach. The stress-induced headaches… I am telling you that I am exhausted because you probably would never notice. I have learned how to carry myself well while grieving internally. So I push through. I have mastered looking well, even when I am not ok. So I push through. My history and my ancestors have taught me that I do not get the privilege of excuse-making. So I push through…

We as Blacks do not need one additional source of exhaustion, given that living in America and surviving inequity is tiring in and of itself. Living in the past or focusing on the future is an additional source of exhaustion that we absolutely do not need. The good news is that there are ways to learn mindfulness skills to help us focus more on the here and now.

Here is an exercise that can help African Americans practice staying present while also acknowledging the effect racial slights have on us. As persons of color, many of us experience overt racial slights and microaggressions. Microaggressions are comments or actions that express a prejudiced attitude toward a member of a marginalized group (such as a racial minority). These slights can be intentional or unintentional. When a microaggression happens to us, we sometimes try to avoid it, blank it out, focus on it in length, under-react to it, or overreact to it. We may become tense, anxious, depressed, angry, shocked, or exhausted in response. We may carry those feelings long after the event has happened. Or, we may maintain tension and anxiety around those who have potential bad behavior, anticipating that another microaggression may occur in the future.

Please know that this exercise is not purposed for you to accept microaggressions or see them as okay behavior toward you; microaggressions and racial slights are specific types of bad behavior. In addition, this exercise is not about the person insulting you—it is about helping you! It was created and adapted based on an activity by Matthew Boone (Stoddard & Afari 2014, 102–103).

EXERCISE: Racial Slights and Staying Present

A worksheet for this exercise is also available at http://www.newharbinger.com/49883.

If you are willing, I invite you to do an exercise to acknowledge racial slights and help you practice staying present. I'd like you to come up with an object in the room that represents a racial slight or microaggression that happened to you. It can be a ball, a rock, a marker, an index card—anything. As you look at the object, recall a specific racial incident. Know that you cannot wish the object away because the incident did happen. Focus on the object for a while as you think about it representing that racial incident.

Notice how you feel as you focus on the racial-slight object. What kinds of feelings are you having right now? As you focus on the object, what types of feelings are you having in your body? Can you describe them?

Don't try to push these feelings away, and do not focus on the person who insulted you. Instead, focus on the feelings and sensations you are having right now as you look at the racial-slight object. Know that the feelings and thoughts you are having are normal. Anyone would feel these feelings if they experienced a put-down or a slight.

Now, I want you to realize that that object and what was said to you has no real power in your life today. Because that slight happened then, and it is not happening right now. That racial slight does not define who you are now. It does not identify you. It was a past microaggression by someone with bad behavior. But that object, that racial slight, is not tied to your present in any way. It is not linked to your values. Those hurtful words do not define you.

You can exhale and release the weight of those words. You need not waste time and effort trying to figure the bad actor out. The words have no power at this moment.

Now that you realize that this racial slight is not tied to your present life, how do you feel? How does your body feel?

By staying in the present, we are freer to act and move toward our own values, goals, and desires. Being stuck in the past or straining toward the future does nothing except exhaust us further. In the next chapter, "More Than What I've Been Through"—Self-as-Context, we will discuss how while we are a product of our past, we are so much more than that. We will learn how we can let go of the "damaged goods" mantra and begin to see ourselves as much more than the trials, tribulations, and experiences we go through.

CHAPTER 6

"More Than What I've Been Through"— Self-as-Context

It isn't where you come from: it's where you're going that counts.

—Ella Fitzgerald

"I am not interested in counseling. What can a counselor say to me?" Trinity barked to her friend Brianna.

Brianna was worried about Trinity. They were friends since elementary school, brought up in the same neighborhood in Milwaukee. Brianna was so close to Trinity over the years that it was like they were family. As children, Trinity would stay over at Brianna's house with her family for weeks at a time, especially when it got bad at Trinity's house. That was most of the time.

Trinity's mother had struggled with drug addiction from the time Trinity was five years old. Even at a young age, Trinity had times when she had to make her own meals because her mom was gone for two or three days at a time. At age seven, Trinity once almost set the apartment on fire when she tried to make a meal for herself. She got rewarded with the beating of her life by her mother, who just happened to come back early that day. Most days, the refrigerator and cupboards were bare. There were times when she was nine and ten that strangers would regularly come to the house to see her mother. She would hear her mother groaning in the bedroom and the bed squeaking in the one-bedroom apartment during those times. The walls were paper-thin, and Trinity tried to cover her ears during those times, but she still could hear the sounds. When Trinity was ten, one of the strangers didn't leave before raping Trinity. Trinity's mom was in the corner of the bedroom, nodding off as it happened.

It was after this that Trinity stayed at Brianna's house more and more. Brianna's parents felt terrible for Trinity and welcomed her to stay when she liked. They knew Trinity was neglected. However, Trinity had kept the sexual and physical abuse incidents in her life to herself.

When Trinity was fifteen, her mother got arrested for drug possession and received a sentence of five years in prison. Because the apartment rent was not being paid anymore, Brianna knew that Trinity would be out on the streets if she didn't stay with them. So, Brianna's family took her in, and she fully lived with them from age fifteen to finish high school in a stable environment.

But now, both girls were almost eighteen years old, and they were graduating from high school soon. Brianna had worked hard in school and she got offers to attend three different colleges, along with scholarship offers. Trinity, though, never thought about a plan after high school, and anytime Brianna or her family tried to talk to Trinity about it, Trinity shut them down.

A day before Trinity's eighteenth birthday (three months before graduation), Trinity got so drunk that she slept with two guys at a party she attended. She did not come home until 4 a.m. When she returned to Brianna's home and was asked about her whereabouts, Trinity cursed out Brianna's parents. Brianna's parents, telling her how disrespectful her behavior was toward them, gave Trinity an ultimatum. Trinity needed to be out of their house after graduation. Brianna would be off to college that summer, and Trinity could not stay much longer with the family.

The family was willing to pay for counseling for Trinity, which Trinity adamantly refused over the past three years she was living with them. After the birthday incident, Brianna said, "Maybe you should get some counseling, Tri. You never really dealt with everything you went through as a kid."

Trinity responded, "I'm not interested in counseling. What can a counselor say to me that I don't already know? That I'm a slut, a loser, a fuck-up? That I'm useless and destined to be a hooker on the streets like my mom? Screw getting a counselor," she angrily replied.

Damaged Goods

Trinity's story is heartbreaking. She had to take care of herself as an adult at a developmental age and stage when she needed someone to care for her. She was in an environment that was dangerous and unpredictable. She was violated physically by her own mother, and when she was molested, she had no protection. It makes sense that she might feel lost or distrustful of the world based on what she has endured.

Somewhere along the way, she began to identify herself and her essence as her mother's trajectory. Over time, she developed the idea that she was damaged, ineffective, useless, flawed, and unlovable. That she did not deserve to go to college or to have a "normal" life. That she was destined for a life where she used her body to get by like her mother did. She never expected to have a healthy relationship with a man because she felt she did not deserve it.

Regardless of the trauma experienced, when we think of ourselves as damaged goods, we believe that something is wrong with us that cannot be fixed. A person is considered damaged goods when they are seen as flawed, spoiled, or irreparably broken. When we are labeled as damaged goods, our character and even our worth is in question." Damaged goods has a very negative connotation to it; a person who is damaged goods is considered to be no longer desirable or valuable because of something that has happened to them. Those who are considered damaged goods have damaged reputations. We believe we are hiding a monster behind our skin that people would shriek and run from if they only knew that monster was really there. We feel that we have an irreversible and irreparable flaw deep within ourselves. We feel worthless. We look in the mirror and don't like what we see because we see a broken person.

Sometimes, we get things twisted, and the things that happen to us begin to define us. Or the things that people have said to us become us. "You're stupid." "You're a loser." "I wish you were never born." These statements toward us begin to define us, and we start to identify with them. We can be removed from dysfunctional environments, as Trinity was at age fifteen. The sad thing is that we can look functional and dress functional and behave functional, yet we can still define ourselves based on what we've been through and not who we are now.

When we start to define our lives based on past experiences, we stop seeing our whole selves (good and bad) and only see the bad. We begin to engage in the self-fulfilling prophecy. Because we see ourselves as damaged, we engage in behavior that damaged people would engage in. If we define ourselves as a slut, we engage in conduct that could be considered sexually loose. If we define ourselves as stupid, we give up immediately at the sign of any challenge because we feel that we are not smart enough. As we believe the mantra "There's something wrong with me," we hold off on life and every positive thing until we are fixed. Yet, we believe that we cannot be repaired, so that day never comes.

It feels so alone and so lonely to accept the "I'm damaged" mantra. We feel like everyone else is "normal" while we are not. We feel like we are the only ones who have dealt with such trauma, and no one else could possibly understand. We may feel judged by our family or friends when, in reality, we are judging ourselves. So, we may isolate ourselves or put a wall up to protect ourselves from others, shutting ourselves in through the process.

When we see ourselves as broken and damaged, we cannot see a positive future for ourselves. We cannot see past the damage if we *are* the damage. This view pervades our entire life. We may primarily have thoughts that coincide with our view of ourselves as damaged. We may have only sadness or anger because we do not deserve happiness or joy if we are damaged. Spiritually we may also be lost because we may feel that no God would allow things to happen to us so traumatizing or unfair. And if there is a God, that means that God doesn't love everyone. "Especially someone damaged like I am."

Is the Damaged Goods Mantra a Black American Mantra?

Damaged-goods thinking has not been thrust upon any set of people more thoroughly than Blacks in America. Only we, of all races that make up the tapestry of America, were considered goods, property, something to be owned. Thus, the "goods" of damaged goods are very significant in our lives. We were the only "Americans" with forefathers who were dragged and brought here against their will, enslaved for nearly three hundred years. We were the only Americans born with questions and a feeling of being lost—the lack of belonging—to a country that we never actually belonged in. Africa is but a distant ancestral memory, given that our families were torn apart. It makes sense that some, if not many of us, may feel like damaged goods.

There are cycles of oppression that continue in a never-ending process, where "the powerful oppress those less powerful, who in turn oppress those even less powerful than they" (DeGruy 2005, IV). Thus, some cause damage through oppression and abuse, and those who have experienced that damage then hurt others. My pastor would always say, "Hurt people hurt other people." Thus, the damaged goods issue is complicated.

I suspect that Trinity's mother was hurt or traumatized by circumstances herself. That, in turn, led her to her own actions—using drugs, prostitution, neglect, and abuse of her child. Trinity's mother passed on her trauma and pain down to Trinity. And if the cycle of oppression is not broken, it can very likely be that Trinity will pass down hurt and pain to her own children.

This damaged goods mantra, for Blacks, is not just internal. From the time we are born, we constantly hear messages about how inferior we are. We listen to them on the media. For instance, as a child, my mother and I used to count the times that a reporter mentioned the race of a criminal assailant if that criminal was Black. If the criminal was Black, his race was almost always mentioned. If the criminal was white, they did not even state it most times, as if race was a non-issue in those cases. What occurred was that criminality was attached to the Black race, even when many criminals were not Black.

The damaged goods mantra is inherent in our legal fight to have natural Black hairstyles seen as "businesslike" or professional. What other race has had to fight legally to respect their natural hair in the business and professional world? As a young child, I remember how I was told that I needed to get my hair "pressed" or put chemicals in my hair for it to be straightened so that I could fit into the mainstream world. Intellect, talent, and experience are not located in hair follicles or in our outside appearance. Why, then, have we been pressured to assimilate and to minimize or ignore our ancestral attributes? To make our hair straighter or our skin lighter or get nose jobs to attempt to change our nose shapes. The damaged goods mantra is prevalent when it comes to minimizing or belittling our natural appearance.

The damaged goods mantra is unconsciously taught to police officers who racially profile and criminalize our Black boys. The damaged goods mantra shows up in court when judges make racist rulings based simply on race.

The damaged goods mantra has prevailed in medicine and in psychology. In medicine, Blacks have been seen as having the ability to handle more pain. This is not empirical truth. Instead, this idea stems from slavery, where pain was thrust upon Blacks through whippings, mutilation, imprisonment, torture, and other types of punishments. In psychology, research was done to erroneously attempt to prove that Black people were less intelligent and were inferior.

The damaged goods mantra has been delegated to us regarding the way that we speak. Individuals scoff and joke about Ebonics, labeling African American speech as inferior. However, English was purposefully taught incorrectly to enslaved Africans by enslavers, who wanted to create a differentiation between the two races. This was to support their notion that Blacks were inferior and less than. Enslavers punished Black people who attempted to learn to read and write. They discouraged and admonished the education of anyone with darker skin. Thus, the way that African Americans speak among one another evolved over time. Through academic institutions and other means, we have been conditioned to assimilate. We have been taught that Eurocentric Americanized English is the proper way to speak, while culturally influenced speech is inferior, ignorant, and damaged.

Brown skin is looked at as a deficit, a threat, something to be minimized or ignored. We *are* damaged goods, the messages say. We are violent. We are always angry. We are volatile. We are useless. We should be pitied.

I love Dr. Joy DeGruy's book, where she lays out Post-Traumatic Slave Syndrome. It is vital to understand our history to see why intergenerational pain perpetuates in our families. I will not go too deep into how trauma works. However, it has been researched and shown that trauma (physical, emotional, psychological, or spiritual injuries) critically affects our biology through our DNA. And if trauma causes a biological impact, that means that trauma can be intergenerational, passed down from one generation to the next.

So, what happened to us, given the trauma from over four hundred years of slavery and racism? Has there been any significant movement toward addressing that trauma in our lives? Since there has been no specific healing process available, what have we done as Black people? We adapted so that we could survive. But our views about ourselves? That damaged goods mantra is prevalent and pervasive. Resultant thoughts from our adaptation process include:

- "The only ones of my people who really make it in this world are people who play sports and sometimes music."

- "At least in jail, I get three hots and a cot."

- "I am just happy that I at least woke up this morning."

- "It is impossible for a Black person to be successful in America."

- "We are already seen as lazy losers based on the color of our skin, so why bother?"

- "Life goal? I don't even see myself living past age eighteen."

There is a portion of Dr. Joy DeGruy's book that really brings this damaged-goods thinking home. Damaged-good thinking was *adaptive* in a system of slavery because it was *protective*.

When we roll the scene back a few hundred years, we see a slave master walking through the fields and coming upon an enslaved woman. He approaches her and her children and remarks, "Well now—that Mary of yours is really coming along." The mother, terrified that the slave master may see qualities in her daughter that could merit her being raped or sold, says, "Naw, sir, she ain't worth nothin'. She cain't work. She's stupid. She's shiftless." (DeGruy 2017)

To preserve her daughter's virginity and keep her daughter with her, the mother labeled her daughter as damaged goods to protect her. Imagine being in a situation where you had to belittle your child to protect them. We do not have to go far to imagine this because it still happens today. I think of Trayvon Martin's mother (Trayvon died at age seventeen), and Eric Rice's mother (Eric died at age twelve), and Elijah McClain's mother (Elijah died at age twenty-three). I think of the mothers of thousands of Black children and young adults who have been unjustly killed in the last two decades, as well as the hundreds of thousands in the last few centuries. I understand how a Black mother might try to keep their little Black boys and girls little for as long as possible for fear of them being seen as a threat or a sexual target. "Rayshawn is just thirteen. He's still really young. He's really innocent. He doesn't know much. He's just a kid." All for the purposes of protection.

This damaged goods mantra is particularly complicated and ingrained when it comes to African Americans. It is possible, though, that ACT can begin to help with healing. ACT can enable individuals to move from "I am my experiences" to "I am more than my experiences."

Break Past the Damaged Goods Mantra by Going Meta

We have had many experiences in our lives that affected us. And those experiences helped to shape who we have become. However, while those experiences *contributed* to who we are, they are not what we are. The essence of who we really are expands much more extensively and is more profound than our experiences. We are more than our experiences!

ACT discusses something called "self-as-context" to help us understand this. This concept gets a bit theoretical, existential, and high-minded, so my goal is to put it into terms that are more accessible to everyone.

Have you heard the phrase "Go meta"? Going meta can be described as not just doing what I'm doing but looking and observing myself doing what I'm doing. Some of you who are older can remember a comedy show called *Mad TV* (if not, you can Google anything and see it on YouTube). On *Mad TV*, the comedian and actor Keegan-Michael Key (of *Key & Peele* fame) would play a character named Eugene. Eugene would always say, "You know, hey, when I was a kid, I liked [such and such], and it was on this level, but you? You took it to a 'hole... 'nother... level!" I get tickled just thinking about his playing of that role.

Going meta is taking it to that whole other level. We can be stuck in our emotions and thoughts about what has happened to us, or we can learn techniques to go meta.

What can going meta look like? At one time or another, some of us may have experienced an almost "out of body" experience. Sometimes, this happens when someone has experienced a shocking situation or a traumatic event. For instance, it could happen if someone was in a severe car accident. Or, it could have potentially happened to Trinity while she was sexually abused by the stranger in their apartment. In those times, it can feel like we are not even in our body but that we are outside of it or hovering over it, watching a scene in a movie play. The fancy word for this is "depersonalization," or the persistent feeling of observing oneself from outside one's body or having a sense that one's surroundings aren't real. Sometimes, this happens to the body as an automatic protective mechanism. It could have been too much for Trinity to handle as a child to be "in the moment" while being raped, so her body may have kicked into a different gear. She may have felt detached from her body while the pain was at its highest.

Depersonalization is not the same as going meta. Still, it can help us to understand what going meta might look like. If a person can go meta, they may be able to observe themselves and talk about their past, present, and future. The person may be able to do this without feeling as if they are in the event they are discussing. It is like going to a concert to see yourself on stage, yet you are watching yourself from the balcony.

Russ Harris explained self-as-context (going meta) in plain language in his book ACT Made Simple (Harris 2019, 289):

> Self-as-context is the part of you that does all the noticing. Metaphorically, it's like (a) a "safe place" inside you, where you can "open up" and "make room" for difficult thoughts and feelings, and (b) a "perspective" or "viewpoint" from which to "step back" and observe thoughts and feelings.

So how is going meta different from depersonalization? While depersonalization happens on reflex, as a result of being in severe trauma, going meta is a choice and can be learned. Depersonalization occurs to protect someone from a trauma happening right at that time. However, the purpose of going meta is not to protect oneself but instead to free oneself from thoughts such as "I am damaged goods." When we purposefully go meta, we begin to see parts of our life differently, as if we were watching in the audience rather than being in the game. By going meta, we can begin to notice and observe thoughts, feelings, and events in our life without being reactionary. And by going meta, we start to learn that we are much greater than our circumstances and our past.

The essence of who we are stretches across time and is much grander and more significant than the events in our lives. So, going meta is actually a good thing. We want to get to a place where we understand that our self-concept, self-image, and essence of who we are—they are *greater*. Our essence is greater than what the media portrays we are. It is greater than skin color itself. It is greater than the sum total of all negative experiences we have had. It is even greater than our ancestors experienced. While we honor and cherish our ancestors, what they had to go through to survive, and how they sacrificed for us, the essence of who we are is even greater than that. In other words, the nature of who we really are does not stop at the door of what our ancestors experienced. This is excellent news because you are valuable. You are worthy. You are here for a reason and a purpose. You, like all humans, deserve good things. You belong, even if others say you don't. You are enough. You were made perfectly right, even with your flaws.

However, just saying mantras of positive affirmations is not enough. By going meta, we can learn self-awareness to begin to believe the truth about who we really are. Here is how you do it:

- Going meta is like you watching yourself at a concert or movie. Stop what you are doing for a moment and notice some things happening in the movie right now.

- Notice your feelings right now.

- Notice how your body feels.

- Notice the thoughts that are whizzing through your head right now.

- Notice your body sitting in the chair and what you can see and hear.

- Notice the different details of your movie and that there's a part of you that can go meta and step back and notice the movie.

- As you watch this movie, remember that this is just a tiny part of the movie and that you are bigger and more significant than the movie.

Let's go back to Trinity's case to see how going meta can help. A great thing happened to Trinity: she eventually agreed to accept Brianna's parents' offer. She started counseling with an ACT therapist before her graduation. Trinity was fearful about going to therapy because she did not want to be asked many questions about the sexual abuse that she had endured or about her mother. They were touchy subjects for her. She was happy to discover that her therapist had no intention of grilling her about her past or of trying to place blame on her for her behaviors. The ACT therapist worked with Trinity about her damaged-goods feelings during one particular session.

Trinity: (looking anxious and angry) I know I only have so much time left to stay at the house I'm staying in. But I just don't think it is fair for people to expect me to be like Brianna. She was always smart; everyone knew she was going to college. So, what am I supposed to do? How could they expect that of me? That really pisses me off.

Therapist: Trinity, this is a great place to see if you can go meta here. (Here, the therapist engages in an exercise with Trinity to go meta.)

Trinity: Ok, I'm going meta now. Yea, I'm bigger than this movie. (She sighs)

Therapist: I heard an exhale. Can you tell me more about that?

Trinity: I just felt a weight lift off me. When I remembered that I'm more than just this situation and went meta. So, that's why I sighed.

Therapist: Ok! Now, I wonder if you would be willing to do an exercise with me about your reaction to what your mind is telling you.

Trinity: Sure, if it's not too deep. (She laughs).

Therapist: Suppose your mind told you, "I can't go to college like Brie because I'm broken and stupid, and she's not." What happens if you get completely hooked by that thought and go through each day convinced that you have no chance of college or a good job because you are broken? As you connect to that thought, what happens to the people that matter to you and your relationship with them—Brianna and her parents—who you said that you loved?

Trinity:	Well, I guess I spend a lot of time away from them all because I don't think I deserve to be with them.
Therapist:	And what if you had the thought that "If something happens to fix me, then I will be worthy of college, a good job, and relationships." What happens as you wait to be fixed?
Trinity:	What do you mean what happens? Oh—nothing happens. I'm just waiting.
Therapist:	And what happens to the relationships that you care about, and to your own life, as you wait?
Trinity:	I lose my relationships. And nothing gets done.
Therapist:	(pulls out a blank sheet of paper) Okay. If you're willing, let's write down some of the things you say to yourself about being damaged. I'm broken. I'm damaged. I don't deserve love or goodness until I am fixed. I am different from those I care about. (The therapist continues with Trinity to fill out the sheet, also asking about anything she learned culturally about herself that caused her to feel like damaged goods).
Therapist:	Now, if you are willing, please hold this paper up in front of your face so you can read all of the comments about being damaged goods. Hold it tightly.
Trinity:	(Holding the paper up, cutting off the therapist from her view)
Therapist:	So, Trinity, you have a tight hold on this damaged goods mantra. Can you see anything besides what you are holding onto tightly?
Trinity:	No, I can only see this.

Therapist:	Now imagine that right in front of you is everything important to you. Your relationship with your friend and friend's family, your desires for your future career. While you hold tightly to these damaged goods stories about yourself, what happens to everything important to you?
Trinity:	I can't see any of it.
Therapist:	Do you feel connected or engaged with anything important to you?
Trinity:	Nope. I just feel like I'm on hold.
Therapist:	Now, put the paper down on your lap (Trinity does so). When the damaged goods story is not in front of you, can you connect or engage with what is important to you?
Trinity:	Yea, I think so.
Therapist:	So, given that you are more significant than the story being told, are you willing to move toward what you care about whether you think that you are "fixed" or not?
Trinity:	"I can try, I think." (Adapted from the Good Self/ Bad Self Exercise, 298–300).

By reading this dialogue, perhaps you can see a wonderful thing about ACT. There is no expectation of perfection, of being "fixed." Instead, ACT helps us live one day at a time toward our values, toward what matters to us.

Trinity has begun to take steps toward what and who she cares about. This is not a Cinderella story, but neither are our lives. There is not necessarily an "and she lived happily ever after moment." Our past is still our past, and racism and challenges will still present themselves in our lives. But Trinity has begun to see herself differently, and she no longer waits to live life when she is undamaged. Step by step, she has already started to make decisions that will move her toward her values, toward acceptance of love from her friends, loved ones, and most importantly, herself.

A move toward what you care about does not have to be gigantic for it to count. It can be big or small. Day by day, decision by decision, if you learn how to move toward your own values, that is a success. You no longer have to wait to live life—you can live life each day, even through pain, as you move toward what matters to you.

If you have a history of trauma, you may have become attached to a conceptualized self that is on guard, distrustful, or isolating. Yet you value closeness and intimacy in relationships. The following exercise can help you see that self-protection during trauma can be good. Still, continuing to protect yourself long after the trauma has occurred can be damaging. The metaphor "Boxing 24/7" is adapted from "Taking Off Your Armor" by David Gillanders, which is in *The Big Book of ACT Metaphors* (Stoddard & Afari 2014, 122).

Exercise: Boxing 24/7

A worksheet for this exercise is also available at http://www.newharbinger.com/49883.

You may feel like your life has been one gigantic boxing match, where you have had ongoing hits (pains) and sharp blows (trauma). You may feel like you have had to box with pain or trauma in your early life, hit after hit, that you had to figure out how to defend yourself from. There might have been a slap or punch from people who were supposed to protect you and care for you. Or, you might have been hammered over and over because of the problematic environment or neighborhood you lived in. Possibly you have been physically or mentally bullied. Or maybe you kept getting battered in your education or academic life. Maybe you have felt like you have not caught many breaks in life. Perhaps you experienced racism against you or against your family or loved ones in various ways—blow after blow from the system. And trauma, each traumatic or painful event in your life, may feel like a slap in the face or a punch in a boxing match that you did not ask to be a part of.

So, you might have learned how to fight physically, emotionally, or mentally. You might have ducked and dodged, trying to be like Muhammad Ali ("Float like a butterfly, sting like a bee"). You may have fought and battled for your life preservation, and that is okay! You may have had to fight for your life. Anyone who was in your situation may have likely fought for survival like you did.

The question is, though, do you now define yourself as a fighter—a continual fighter? Have you gotten so comfortable in your protective boxing stance that it is like an extension of your own skin? Have you forgotten that boxing is not a 24/7 profession? Boxers don't fight everyone, only the persons that they are contracted to get into the ring with.

Look at your life right now. Are you imagining fights or potential boxing matches where there are none? Are you continually ready for a fight, with a perpetual chip on your shoulder? In fact, are you instigating some fights—boxing matches in your home, at your job, or with your friends and family? Are you still in a battle with the people around you? Maybe the need for boxing is over (you are no longer in a traumatic situation), but you still have your gloves on emotionally. Perhaps you have drawn an invisible line on the ground, waiting with hands in fists for someone to cross the line emotionally.

Consider how free you are to move and to act without having to fight. What is being on guard all the time really costing you? While it is true that the ability to fight kept you from being hurt, it may have also stopped you from really having the feeling of being held, being loved.

Imagine what it would be like to take off the boxing gloves and lay them down. Are they needed in your life right now?

You have the ability to learn to "go meta" and you can set down the boxing gloves to welcome new experiences in life. Knowing in your heart that you are much more than the experiences that you have can free you from continually feeling like damaged goods. In the next chapter, "Living Our Life Like It's Golden," we will celebrate! You actually can live a life that is beyond just survival. You can live a life that embraces your own values.

CHAPTER 7

"Living Our Life Like It's Golden"—Values

Have a vision. Be demanding.

—Colin Powell

One thing about COVID-19 is that it caused us, collectively, to have the experience of living from situation to situation. Some of us had to deal with our loved ones getting ill from the virus or possibly even sadly dying, and we scrambled to make adjustments. Some of us dealt with quick and immediate financial changes, jobs or businesses being closed or shut down, or having to adjust quickly to working online instead of in person. We had to go through not seeing our extended or even close family members such as our parents, grandparents, daughters, and sons like we used to. We had to adjust quickly to the gyms being closed down, and stores being without toilet paper. And for years after the virus began to spread, many did not take vacations, and we did not go out and about. We put recreation on hold, and some of us had to take care of our children while simultaneously working from home.

The past decades have certainly been tumultuous. The times have been challenging, with increased unemployment, illness, war, systemic racism, terrorism, higher prices, divisive elections of politics, terrorism, and death—yet we survived. We went into survival mode, and we survived.

Putting Out Fires and Living Like We're Lost

Survival mode happens when your paychecks are variable, or when your loved one is unemployed and, for some reason, people do not hire them, or when you are wondering if you will be able to pay your rent or feed your children tomorrow. Because of the inequities of the social determinants of health, survival mode is more likely for underrepresented populations such as African Americans. Survival mode is a learned behavior based upon the situations happening in our lives. If we have more traumatic situations, then we are more likely to be in survival mode. Many African Americans (not all but some) have had to be in this survival mode for a long time. We are trying to survive.

Many of us have not thought through how to move from surviving to thriving. We are so used to putting out fires in our lives, from one crisis to the next, that living toward value has not even been a thought. Some of us cannot even imagine staying alive, like Rodney.

Story: *Survival Is Not a Given*

Rodney was a fifteen-year-old African American male who lived in the Watts community and was court-referred to counseling by the Los Angeles County Probation Department. Rodney was a slightly thin but otherwise average-looking young man. He was gang-affiliated and committed some minor offenses, which led to his present probation and mandated therapy.

Rodney appeared very cooperative during the assessment portion of his meeting with his therapist, Patricia. Thus, Patricia looked forward to the treatment planning and intervention phase of therapy with him. There, she would ask Rodney about his goals and future desires. When she got the opportunity, Patricia asked Rodney, "What do you see yourself doing, or what would you like to be doing when you are over age eighteen?"

Rodney calmly yet immediately answered. "I don't see myself living to age eighteen. Living in my neighborhood? I see myself as being dead long before eighteen."

Patricia didn't know what to say. She was truly stumped.

I am not judging being in survival mode—I am acknowledging that we have needed to survive as Blacks. We have had to be the strong Black woman or the strong Black man because we have had to keep it moving to survive. So, starting to talk about our personal values and how we may potentially move toward them is very refreshing. What is it like living life just trying to get through one crisis after the next, to simply avoid pain? It is like being in a sailboat without a sail. What is the purpose of a sailboat without a sail? It doesn't go anywhere.

Purpose Is the Ultimate Motivator

Before we were brought here to America on slave ships from Africa, I imagine that we had purpose and direction through our culture. But then we were uprooted from that purpose. I do not know about you, but I do not feel like I belong in the United States, although I was born here. I have limited information about my ancestors—my grandparents and great-grandparents and beyond—and I have no understanding of what our ancestors' lives were like before they were brought to this country.

For you, what does it feel like to not belong in a place where you were born? Belonging is so crucial and so important. Action without a clear direction is unstable. We long to know: Why are we here? Why were we born? Was it an accident or a divine plan?

My name is "Jennifer." I looked that up, and it means "white wave, instability." "Tossed to-and-fro." And that may have defined me in earlier years, but it does not define me now. My purpose keeps me on a direct path. My purpose is my ultimate motivator. When storms come in life, and when things get hard, my purpose keeps me from giving up. It is the gasoline in my engine. It is the very breath that gives me life. My purpose is rooted deep in my soul, such that it remains untouched when the storms of life blow. And particularly when life is painful, and I want to avoid—hide, pull the covers over my head, close the shades—my purpose gently guides me, sometimes step by step, sometimes less, toward what matters to me.

I must be completely authentic and admit that I was not always this way. I did not always have a purpose or know my purpose. I cannot tell you precisely how I got to this place in my life where I just have this "knowing" about what I need to accomplish in my own life. I am sure an enormous influence on me is my spirituality and connection with a higher and more significant source than myself. I often talk to people, young and old, who have a puzzled look when I talk about my purpose because they don't have that understanding for themselves. They do not know what their purpose is. They do not have a driving force that leads and guides them. Sometimes they feel angry, envious, guilty, or ashamed when they realize that they do not live with purpose or intention.

I want to talk to each of them, and you also if you feel purposeless. Do not feel shame about not having a purpose. Do not feel guilty about that. Your journey is your own, and no one should judge you if you do not understand why you are here on Earth or what you are here to accomplish. Living life can be desperately hard, and sometimes the trials can feel so burdensome that you may even question your existence. The last thing that you need is to feel guilty about when you feel lost. Whether you have the answers right now or not, you are still you, and you still matter. It is just fine and okay to be you—right here and right now—with or without an understanding of your purpose.

Purpose versus Values

Everyone may not understand their purpose or have a specific purpose that guides them. But everyone has values, whether they are aware of them or not. The essential meaning of the word "purpose" is to have a reason for doing something, a feeling of determination about doing it, and a sense that what you are doing will lead to a goal.

Thus, purpose is intentional and clear. It is a clear direction that someone has, the determination and intent to move toward that over-arching goal. But everyone is not necessarily blessed with that knowledge—and that is entirely okay.

You may be one of those who struggle with questions like, "What am I doing here?" or "Where am I going?" If so, although you may not have the clarity or determination connected with purpose, you do have values. We all have values, even if we have never stated them aloud or consciously thought about them.

When we think of values, we can think about something of value—something that is worth a great deal to you. Something that is extremely important to you or that is desirable to you. Someone might say, "I don't care about anything" or "I don't have anything that is worth anything to care about." But we all have something important to us:

- Maybe it's the relationship we have with our family or friends.

- Perhaps it's having a safe place for our children to sleep at night.

- It could be the idea of freedom, independence, or justice.

- Maybe it is a nostalgic dream about feeling peaceful or joyful during the day instead of feeling stressed.

- Possibly it is just being seen by others, or being loved, or being accepted.

All of us have values, spoken or unspoken, that we find desirable. ACT helps you explore the values that you have. Values are an essential and vital part of the ACT model. "At its heart, values ask *why* when it comes to an action, rather than just *what* the action is. Asking why you are undertaking an activity points to the purpose or the meaning." (Bennett & Oliver 2019, 76).

However, the word "values" itself sometimes invokes various negative feelings in some people. That term turns some people off. You may feel that values = morals, tradition, old-school thinking. Some hear the word "values" and equate that to constraints, rules, or regulations. You may feel shame, guilt, or irritation because you feel like someone in your life—parents, family, and friends—think you should have values, but they think you don't. Or they are convinced that you don't. Some think about the word "values" and think about religious fundamentalists or doctrines shoved down everyone's throats. You could also read the word "values" and think of loved ones you disappointed or mistakes you made.

In addition, you may think about values that have been imposed or placed upon you, like WASP (white Anglo-Saxon Protestant) values. Some people in power in the United States have made assumptions that their values are automatically everyone else's values. And that has turned some African Americans off. Some of us say, "What is the point of having values or goals? Systemic oppression keeps us from getting to them, so why bother?" It is like someone who always feels like they are on the losing end of a team, always an underdog. "What is the point of wasting time on values?," they might say.

What are American values and assumptions? America is an individualistic culture with certain specific values. They can be seen in the constitutional documents, the songs, and the sayings that Americans hold dear. And in each of them, we can also see contradictions and paradoxes when thinking about applying these values to those of African ancestry in America. Here are American words and values that have caused Blacks in America pain because of the disconnect between American values and the Black experience in America:

- From "The Star-Spangled Banner": "O'er the land of the *free* and the home of the *brave*."

- From the Pledge of Allegiance, which every child must learn and recite: "One nation under God…with liberty and justice for all."

- From the Preamble of the Declaration of Independence: "We hold these truths to be self-evident, that *all men are created equal*, that *they are endowed by their Creator with certain unalienable Rights*, that among these are Life, Liberty and the pursuit of Happiness."

- From the Preamble of the US Constitution: "We the People of the United States, in order to form a more perfect Union, *establish Justice, ensure domestic Tranquility*, provide for the common defense, promote the general Welfare, and *secure the Blessings of*

Liberty to ourselves and our Posterity, do ordain and establish this Constitution for the United States of America."

- From the song "My Country Tis' of Thee": ... My country 'tis of thee, sweet land of *liberty*—of thee I sing. *Land where my fathers died* (our fathers died too, but by lynchings and other means), land of the pilgrim's pride (?) from every mountainside, *let freedom ring*.

I bring this up because if we discuss values, we should understand the context of values in which African Americans have existed. America's values are liberty, justice, freedom, and equality, according to what has been written. However, there is such a contradiction between America's stated values (one nation under God, with liberty and justice for all) and the history of America. There is an ongoing paradox and pain of living in a place that promotes values that do not apply to people of color. We can and will discuss personal values, but that discussion must always be within the context of the reality in which we reside, live, and survive.

Living My Life Like It's Golden

In 2004, the well-known American soul and rhythm and blues singer-songwriter Jill Scott released her single "Golden" from her third album *Beautifully Human: Words and Sounds Vol. 2*. Many African Americans know the song well.

EXERCISE: Exploring Your Golden Life

You can take some time here to go to your favorite internet search engine and find the lyrics to "Golden" by Jill Scott. In fact, if you search YouTube for the song, you will not only find the lyrics but you can also listen to the song as well. Take some time here to enjoy the song and its lyrics. How does the song and lyrics make you feel? Spend some time thinking about what living a golden life, as described in the song, might look like for you.

That song elicits a feeling of freedom and joy, which comes from both the beautiful voice of Jill Scott and the lyrics. As I examine those lyrics again, I can imagine that, that is what bliss is for me. To find my freedom as I define it and proudly wear it around my neck. To sing out my freedom, loud and strong, as I strut and high-step toward my destination, whatever that may be. To stroke and hold onto my freedom, knowing I was born into it and that it is a natural part of who I am. To hope that God is proud of me as I live my life like it is golden, with purpose. To move toward what I believe is important and what is valuable to me, not with a whimper but with a roar. I *feel* this song every time I hear it, and I know that others, Black and non-Black alike, feel it as well.

For Black persons, a discussion of what it would be like to "live life like it's golden" for them would be very fruitful. If we can examine and think about what a golden life would be for my family and me, then we can paint a picture for ourselves of that golden life and move toward it. *What does living life like it's golden look like for you?*

Personal Values

We envision our golden life uniquely because what matters to each person is different. Some individuals have many values that set their hearts aflame with desire, while others may have only a few. For some, family is of the utmost importance. For others, things like excellence, integrity, or quality drive them most. For others, faith, authenticity, or personal growth are most important to them. And there are those who do not know what their values are. To these individuals, I say you are just fine right where you are in this process! There is no better time to explore what really matters to you than right now.

EXERCISE: Exploring Your Personal Values

A worksheet for this exercise is available at http://www.newharbinger.com/49883.

Problem-solving	Spirituality	Friendship	Thoughtfulness
Gentleness	Rationality	Openness	Health
Hard work	Boldness	Authenticity	Curiosity
God-mindedness	Simplicity	Transparency	Commitment
Peace	Autonomy	Truth	Responsibility
Helpfulness	Competency	Courtesy	Fun
Creativity	Discipline	Growth	Knowledge
Loyalty	Authority	Beauty	Leisure
Contribution	Virtue	Inclusivity	Nonconformity
Belonging	Honesty	Ecology	Genuineness
Security/ safety	Dependability	Humor	Intimacy
Loving	Courage	Passion	Respect
Wisdom	Originality	Accomplishment	Compassion
Maturity	Power	Ambition	Generosity
Vitality	Wealth	Devotion	Romance

Take some moments to relax in whatever way that works for you. Some people use meditation apps such as Calm, Aura, or Headspace to relax. Others may use soothing music or another relaxation method. After you feel relaxed, begin to look at this list of values. What matters to you most? Look at this list of values and choose those that are most important to you—those that would enable you to live a golden life. Feel free to take your time on this—no need to rush it. Also, note to yourself that there is no right or wrong answer. Choose those values that you truly feel in your heart, rather than those you think you "should" choose.

After identifying those values most important to you, go over that list of essential values and choose the top three to five of the most important. Be free as you engage in this and know that the list is not exhaustive. If there is any value important to you that is not on the list, choose that one instead! Also, know that the values you choose today can always be altered or changed. It is what matters to you that counts. You should settle on three to five personal values to move toward living your golden life.

Now sit with those three to five values in front of you. Think about why these particular values are so important to you. How do these values presently exist in your life? Imagine a scale from zero to ten. On a scale where zero is "not at all" and ten is "all the time," without judgment or self-criticism, how frequently are you living out each of these values that are important to you?

Never Neglect Our Collective Values

There is certainly work to be done with our personal values. However, while Black people typically favor more collective values, many of our values are influenced primarily by individualistic, Eurocentric perspectives. There should be space inside and outside the therapy room to discuss both value orientations.

Values are universal, but values are also culturally shaped. To understand African American cultural values, we have to understand them in the context of their history; history cannot be erased from the discussion. Here are descriptions of some of the communal values we share.

Reconnection and Belonging

Before slavery was abolished, our families were torn apart as parents and children were sold to different people and taken to various geographic areas. Instead of bemoaning their fates, our African American ancestors vowed to find their lost loved ones and, even before the end of slavery, saved money and made plans to find those they had lost and buy their freedom. Thus, *reconnection* is a significant value for many of us, as is *belonging*.

Extended Family

Because our ancestors were continually separated from blood relatives, a practice developed where Blacks started designating friends and loved ones as aunts, uncles, nephews, and nieces (although they were not technically related). This custom has roots in Africa. To be anointed with such a family title was considered an honor, a testament to the high esteem in which the family held the person receiving the honorary title. Thus, *extended family* was and continued to be a value. The saying "It takes a village to raise a child" comes from African roots.

Respecting Elders

The tradition of giving elders in the family the utmost respect was established in Africa and continued during slavery. Sadly, older family members during slavery times—if they were able to live to old age—endured the most indignation, shame, and embarrassment. They were tossed away or killed by enslavers like trash because they were seen as obsolete, unproductive, and good for nothing. Thus, *giving the elderly respect* remained a value with African Americans in captivity and beyond.

Tenacity and Persistence

When slavery ended, many of our newly-free Black ancestors bought land primarily in the Northern states, established businesses, and started working on rebuilding traditional family structures. Odds continued to be against our ancestors due to segregation and few economic opportunities for us as a people. But our ancestors still fought. The tenacity and persistence needed to fight for our rights over the next century instilled the family values we inherited, that reflect incredible strength and courage. So, *tenacity* and *persistence* became collective values that we continue to live out in our daily lives.

Faith and Communal Worship

During the period of slavery, our ancestors found strength and unity through communal worship. Many relied on their faith to give them the inspiration they needed to move forward and remind them of the power of kindness and forgiveness, even in the face of the greatest injustice and cruelty. Of course, not all African Americans are religious. Still, communal worship was a protective factor during slavery and beyond for African Americans. The Black church became a symbol of spiritual freedom and an economic and political place to gather. Thus, for many African Americans, *faith* or *communal worship* became a collective value.

Seven Principles of Nguzu Saba

First introduced by Dr. Maulana Karenga in 1966, Kwanzaa is a cultural tradition created for African Americans that is celebrated from the day after Christmas to New Year's Day each year. Our celebration of Kwanzaa includes an acknowledgment and honoring of its seven principles known as Nguzu Saba. The principles are not to be reflected on one week in the year, however. Instead, these principles are values that African Americans share—they can be included in a discussion on collective values. The word *kwanzaa* is a KiSwahili (Kenyan, Ugandan, and Tanzanian) word meaning "first." The seven principles (*nguzo saba*) of Kwanzaa utilize Kiswahili words and address several of our collective values.

1. **Unity (umoja):** maintaining unity as a family, community, and race of people. Considering our background as people subjected to forced separation from our families of origin through slavery, the value of unity is more important to us than ever. We come from the collectivist culture of Africa, where cooperation is elevated above competition. Yet, we find ourselves in a culture where individualism and competition are praised. With unity

comes power, and we have not had much power over the four-hundred-plus years of being in the United States. Thus, unity can give us a collective voice and moves us toward being connected.

2. **Self-determination (kujichagulia):** defining, naming, creating, and speaking for ourselves. This is the cultural value of persevering and continuing the fight to overcome discrimination and adversity in our day-to-day lives. Determination is just that—a stubborn battle and continued press to create equitable and just environments. It also symbolizes our determination to take control of our future and our destinies. This includes creating and supporting Black-owned businesses in our communities and creating shared wealth, increased jobs, and new sources of income. Dr. Maulana Karenga said it this way:

> In a time in which occupation and oppression of countries and peoples are immorally presented as necessary and even salvational, the principle of Kujichagulia (Self-Determination) rejects this and reaffirms the right of persons and peoples to determine their own destiny and daily lives; to live in peace and security; and to flourish in freedom everywhere.

3. **Collective work and responsibility (ujima):** we are collectively responsible for our achievements and our setbacks. With this value, we can recognize the communal nature of the work that needs to be done toward creating our golden lives. For African Americans, personal values are not enough to heal; we must also embrace collective values. Unlike the American value of capitalistic personal financial growth, this value says we can build and maintain our community together. This value says that we must make our brothers' and sisters' problems our problems and solve them together. Like the saying "No child

left behind," we should not settle for personal wealth and be okay with leaving our brothers and sisters in poverty and pain. The mechanisms of slavery have pitted one against the other. This value says that we need to recognize that we are all one team to recover.

4. **Cooperative economics (ujamaa):** to build and maintain our own stores, shops, and other businesses and profit from them together. This value is self-explanatory. It calls for the Black community to self-define its economic future by building Black-owned cooperatives and enterprises. To create permanent pathways out of poverty and to decrease economic disparities, we need viable economic power. We need cooperative economics to lower the national wage gap between Black and white earnings. Thus, this principle values movement toward establishing direct pathways to financial self-sufficiency in Black communities, for equity's sake.

5. **Purpose (nia):** to make our collective vocation the building and developing of our community, to restore our people to their traditional greatness. One term that stands out for me regarding collective purpose or *nia* is the term "traditional greatness." As a culture, we were and are tied to the traditional greatness of our African ancestors. Thus, the collective purpose discussed here is about restoration, rebuilding, repairing, mending, reinstating, and reestablishing the traditional greatness that we once had before the trauma of slavery was thrust upon us. This takes collective action. Marcus Garvey, a Jamaican-born Black nationalist, civil rights activist, and leader of the Pan-Africanism movement, stated:

> Chance has never yet satisfied the hope of a suffering people. Action, self-reliance, the vision of self and the future have been the only means by which the oppressed have seen and realized the light of their own freedom.

6. **Creativity (kuumba)**: to perform acts that leave our community more beautiful and beneficial than we inherited it. Kuumba celebrates creativity as a value. This creativity, however, has a purpose and direction. It is collective creativity, with the aim of generativity versus stagnation, construction versus destruction, to benefit the community rather than tearing it down. This value embraces that we can channel our creative energies to build and preserve a vibrant and robust community. Something that stands out for me in this principle is that the goal is to leave our community more beautiful and beneficial than how we inherited it. This means that our creativity will leave a legacy for our children and children's children.

7. **Faith (imani)**: the profound belief in and commitment to all that is of value to us as a family, community, people, and culture. As we look back on our African roots and ancestry, we come from traditions that (1) believed in a Creator and (2) believed that creation was positive or good. This is important because, since our forced migration to the United States, we have been taught that being dark-skinned is terrible. But in all African spiritual traditions from Egypt on, it is taught that we are in the image of the Creator. Therefore, our collective faith is not just about a Being more significant than ourselves but is also about faith in ourselves. A faith that we were created, and it was good. A faith that, like all men, we are also created in God's image. Imani is about faith in our capacity as humans to live righteously, self-correct, support, care for, and be responsible for each other. And because we are good and not evil, we can have a faith that we are able, eventually, to create a just and reasonable society. Our oppression does not define us, for we are ultimately good, with our unique contribution to the flow of human history. We can honor and embrace our ancestors and our best traditions as a family and community.

Imani, in a nutshell, means to believe in our Creator, our people, our leaders, and the righteousness and victory of our struggle with all our hearts.

EXERCISE: Exploring Collective Values

Here is a list of collective Black values:

Knowledge	Autonomy	Community
Connection	Authenticity	Freedom
Respect	Truth	Culture
Compassion	Tradition	Empowerment
Justice	Integrity	History
Creativity	Liberty	Ancestry
Economic	Equality	Love
Independence	Justice	Persistence
Faith/Spirituality	Family	Resilience
Restoration	Dignity	Belonging
Courage	Security/Safety	Equity
		Peace

This exercise works best in a group. For example, this exercise could be effective if you do it with your family members as they get together before a Thanksgiving meal or at a family barbeque. Or, the exercise could be done with any village or group of support persons you have. It could be done after with your church members or fraternity/sorority members. You could do the exercise with a group of Black friends, coworkers, or neighbors. The exercise can even be done digitally, where a group of people get together via Zoom or on a social media platform. This exercise can work wherever Blacks congregate.

As a group, examine the list of values provided above and have a conversation about what values matter most to the group. Set some ground rules beforehand, noting that every person in the group should be heard and their opinion respected. What are the collective values that matter to the group most? As you collectively identify values, have each group member select their top three values and explain to the group why they are most important. Together, identify a list of a few values that most agree are very important to address. This work will set the stage for committed collective action, which will be discussed in the following chapter.

In conclusion, identifying the personal and collective values that are matter deeply to us is extremely important. Only after identifying our values can we move toward attaining them. We can live life like it is golden by moving toward our values one step, one action at a time. In the next chapter, "Getting It Done—Committed Action," we put these values into action.

CHAPTER 8

"Getting it Done"— Committed Action

I have learned over the years that when one's mind is made up, this diminishes fear; knowing what must be done does away with fear.

—Rosa Parks

Keisha sat incredulous and defeated in front of the judge as he gave custody of her five-year-old son, James, to his father, Ivan. The worse scenario she could have ever imagined was here.

Keisha met and started seeing Ivan starting eight years ago. Ivan initially presented to Keisha as very attentive toward her. He would call or text her throughout the day and they would talk for hours on the phone at night. Ivan made Keisha feel special. Ivan was white and Keisha was Black, but their race did not matter to them when it came to being together. Things progressed between them very fast, and in a few months, Ivan proposed.

It wasn't until after they were married that Keisha began to suspect that Ivan's attentiveness was really jealousy. Ivan began to accuse Keisha of cheating on him. Once, when she returned from the grocery store, Ivan was sitting in the living room in the dark, angrily waiting for her. Ivan punched her, and that was when the domestic violence started in their relationship. Ivan became more and more controlling. Keisha had to look down at all times when anyone else was present, especially other men. She had to wear a watch with a timer and only had a certain amount of time to grocery shop. She would face Ivan's wrath if things did not go his way.

The physical abuse incidents intensified, and Keisha endured spousal rape and regular beatings. Keisha became pregnant, but the abuse continued. Keisha began to try to think of a way to escape, fearing for her own life and the life of her unborn baby. Somehow, Keisha was able to escape and she went to a domestic violence shelter. Ivan's possessiveness escalated, and he began to make threats against her life and threats to hurt loved ones like her mother and sister. Keisha had to go into hiding and her family members moved because of their fear of Ivan.

Flash forward a few years later: Keisha had birthed their baby, James, during the time that she was in hiding. Due to her abuse experiences during pregnancy, James was born prematurely and at three years old has some developmental delays and intellectual disabilities. Now Keisha is trying to go through the process of getting a divorce from

Ivan. Ivan has not taken care of James in the past, has not asked for visits, and has not ever shown concern about James's disabilities. Still, Ivan told Keisha that he plans on getting custody of James "just to show you what a bitch you really are."

During the divorce process, a white male judge oversees the divorce proceeding. This judge clearly favors Ivan over Keisha, stating to Keisha "I don't trust you." This judge overlooks, on purpose, the past domestic violence record, saying, "That's in the past." This judge refuses to listen to Keisha and Keisha's lawyer. And every time that Keisha is in front of this judge, he treats her dismissively, saying, "I don't trust you." Each time that Keisha must go to court, the judge places unreasonable burdens on Keisha as if she were the villain rather than the victim.

And now the day she dreaded and hoped wouldn't or couldn't happen is here. Because a judge finds Keisha contemptible (why?) and favors Ivan, he has created every obstacle necessary for Keisha to maintain physical custody of James. Keisha knows that if Ivan were Black instead of white, he would have been immediately jailed for the domestic violence he perpetrated against her. If Ivan were Black, he likely would have had to have his parental rights terminated. But because Keisha is Black, she is now seen as the suspect in the judge's eyes. White privilege strikes again, to a disabled child's detriment. And another woman of color is severely hurt by the American court system.

Keisha feels hopeless. She knows there is nothing she can do to look different in this judge's eyes. He has viewed her as committing crimes that she did not commit due to the color of her skin. Committed action in this case feels like a whispered dream.

"I did all I could. Years of fighting in the court system. I just can't do it anymore. You know how hard I have tried. I have done everything in my power to keep myself and my baby safe, and I still get, 'I don't trust you.' My baby is being snatched from me, like the babies of our ancestors were snatched from them and sold. It's just a present-day form of that. What else can I do? I'm tired of fighting a system that is not for me."

The "I Don't Trust You" Mantra

What does it mean when judges, and police officers, and politicians, and lawyers, and social workers tell a Black person, "I don't trust you" after seeing them? What can that person say or do to convince them to be seen differently? Keisha just wanted to be heard in the courtroom. How many other Black lives have stood before that judge, or judges like him, every day?

"I don't trust you." The mantra many of us hear daily. "I don't trust you," as a shop owner follows you while you are shopping. "I don't trust you," as someone crosses the street to avoid your path when you are Black, and they are not, and see you coming. "I don't trust you," said silently to your sons and daughters as they sit in their classes at school. "I don't trust you" as they raise their eyebrows, realizing that you are not the housekeeper at the university or hospital; you are the doctor. "I don't trust you" on the job when you wear your hair natural or braided. It's as if people insist that the less you look like them, the more they distrust you.

And "I don't trust you" automatically turns into "I don't see you." "I don't hear you." The sound of your voice and what you are saying are not coming through because they just can't see past the way you look. And devastation results from that.

How do we deal with the repercussions of "I don't trust you"? With the windfall, damage, and domino effect of those four words? What do we do with them? If I were to do an ACT exercise exploring those words and their repercussions in the lives of Blacks, I would ask if you could describe those words as if they were physical, three-dimensional matter or objects; what would they look like to you?

Of course, there is no limit on how different Blacks might see these words. For Keisha, she saw the words physically as a Black, dirty blindfold that some people put on before talking to her. Some might see those words represented by the knee on George Floyd's neck that secured him down to the curb, or as a verbal noose where our ancestors faced physical ones. The words and beliefs "I don't trust you" are stifling, restricting, choking, and controlling. "I don't trust you" leads to "I can't breathe," physically, emotionally, legally, mentally, politically, and even sometimes spiritually.

The "I don't trust you" mantra Keisha and many of us experience is exhausting to fight continuously. Fighting against the system to get your needs met is *tiring*! It is like being a salmon who constantly must swim upstream—not just at certain times of a reproductive cycle, but *all the time*.

Some Blacks in America, like Keisha, can give up fighting because of the energy it takes to fight against ongoing racism, discrimination, and the inequities that are described in the social determinants of health model (discussed in the first chapter). Many of us are "hella tired, no joke." I understand that we need an extra push of energy, drive, whatever you call it, for us to keep going and move from surviving to thriving. Action is much more difficult for those fighting an unjust system—difficult, but not impossible.

Committed Action

Amid all this, if "living life like its golden" is our direction, *committed action* is each active step we take to move toward living that golden life. Committed action can look like starting to do things that we were not doing before, such as exercising ten minutes a day if we desire to be healthier. Or setting up a time to ask our boss for the raise we deserve. Or, committed action can look like stopping a behavior or holding back (Bennett and Oliver 2019, 79). For instance, it could look like holding off from drinking that glass of wine after dinner or taking a social media break to make time for other things more worthwhile to you.

These behaviors do not occur alone. For instance, while deciding to turn off social media for a while, you may also be engaging in other parts of the ACT process that we have discussed. You may exercise being *in the here and now* without social media, making room for any uncomfortable feelings, and just allowing yourself to feel them. You may become more aware of *it is what it is*—you may become more actively "woke" to your present-day life and what is around you. In other words, with committed action, you may not only engage in an activity of choice but you may also work on the other beneficial elements of the ACT model as well.

Committed action and willingness go hand in hand. We have to be willing to move toward what makes our life golden—willingness comes before movement. In my own life, I have found that committed action and courage go together as well. It takes courage to move forward and do something, especially when we do not know how that "something" will turn out. I am saying this because moving forward does not mean we will not still have obstacles or opposition.

If we move forward and ask our boss for that well-deserved raise, there is no guarantee that they will say yes. But the process of moving forward is our victory, not the outcome. If we take even one small step toward our golden life, then that is a step that we can celebrate. Committed action is taken willingly and courageously, leaning into our dreams despite present or potential pain. Committed action is getting it done, whatever that "it" personally is for you. The famed tennis player Arthur Ashe—the only Black man to ever win the singles title at Wimbledon, the US Open, and the Australian Open—said, "Success is a journey, not a destination. The doing is often more important than the outcome." We often want desperately to be already living our golden life. But the journey toward our golden life—getting there—can be much more critical in developing our character than arriving.

Bone Dry and On Empty

I shared earlier that I had to go on public assistance while in my master's degree program because I had to take summers away from my job to attend field placement and classes full-time. And I had two children and a husband who was unable to contribute financially. I will never forget what it was like in the welfare office. I remember how the eligibility workers and security guards looked—tired, worn, and irritable. I remember how they treated the patrons. They snapped at them or dismissed them from the start of their day—when they came in through the metal detectors—until they left the building. I waited for hours and hours even though I had a specific appointment time, and others were waiting for hours and hours too.

What struck me most was that everyone acted as if this was okay. It was okay to be treated this way. It was okay to wait for hours and hours for a specific appointment, only to be told, snappily, that they needed another paper or document and to come back. It was okay to try to call into the office any time of day and get no response. I am not bashing the eligibility workers—the whole system works in this manner, and everyone who is a part of the system seems to think it is okay.

I remember one mother's face as she held her newborn in that dirty office for hours. She appeared so defeated. I knew that my visits to the welfare office were temporary, but those who had less opportunity than I seemed resigned to whatever treatment they received. That felt like learned helplessness to me. I dislike the term "learned helplessness" when applied to people. It sounds defeatist and brings up images of hopelessness, disability, powerlessness, and giving up. However, this concept does at least in part relate to the African American experience.

Let's talk more deeply about the term "learned helplessness" as applied to Blacks in America. Learned helplessness is defined in psychology as:

A mental state in which an organism is forced to bear aversive stimuli, or stimuli that are painful or otherwise unpleasant, becomes unable or unwilling to avoid subsequent encounters with those stimuli, even if they are "escapable," presumably because it has learned that it cannot control the situation. (Seligman 1972, 408)

To explain this definition more clearly, I will go directly to the originator of the concept of learned helplessness and his story. Learned helplessness was discovered accidentally by the psychologists Martin Seligman and Steven F. Maier. They had initially observed helpless behavior among dogs classically conditioned to expect an electrical shock after hearing a tone.

Later, the dogs were placed in a shuttle box that contained two chambers separated by a low barrier. The floor was electrified on one side and not on the other. The dogs previously subjected to classical conditioning made no attempts to escape, even though avoiding the shock simply involved jumping over a small barrier. To investigate this, the researchers then devised another experiment: In group one, the dogs were strapped into harnesses for some time and then released. In group two, the dogs were placed in the same harnesses, but were subjected to electrical shocks that could be avoided by pressing a panel with their noses. In group three, the dogs received the same shocks as those in group two, except that those in this group could not control the shock. For those dogs in the third group, the shocks seemed completely random and outside their control.

The dogs were then placed in a shuttle box. Dogs from the first and second groups quickly learned that jumping the barrier eliminated the shock. Those from the third group, however, made no attempts to get away from the shocks. Due to their previous experience, they had developed an expectation that nothing they did would prevent or eliminate the shocks.

Blacks in America have been, and continue to be, subjected to adverse conditions such as racism, discrimination, and inequities in the social determinants of health. Thus, we may feel that we have no or minimal control over our lives. Therefore, it makes sense that some Blacks may feel helpless and may have developed a pattern of inaction to cope with their situation. When people think that they have *no control* over their situation, they may start behaving helplessly. This *inaction* can lead people to overlook opportunities for relief or change.

"Learned helplessness" is a term that has a negative connotation, especially when applied to African Americans. But many of us can identify with what it feels like to be living on "empty," living life as bone dry as the desert. What does living bone dry and empty look like in African Americans? It might look like someone who fails to ask for help because they feel as if they have had to do things alone anyway, and they may have a hard time trusting the altruism of others. It might look like a child or adult with very low frustration tolerance who gives up at the first sign of resistance or difficulty. It might look like someone who has completely given up trying. It may look like someone who expresses that they are bone-tired and that every effort they give feels overwhelming as if they are moving in molasses. Living bone dry and empty could look like someone who says yes to many things they should say no to, including toxic relationships and people. It could look like someone who is extremely passive, or on the other hand, it could look like someone extremely volatile and aggressive—neither of whom have learned how to be assertive for what counts in their lives. It could look like someone who has no thought about their values or what they care about, or someone who does have values, but is unmotivated to achieve them. Or, it could look like someone who continually procrastinates, distracts, or self-medicates to avoid thinking about what matters to them because they do not believe that they could ever get what matters to them anyway.

Learned helplessness, depression, and racial discrimination go hand in hand. Madubata and colleagues (2018) showed that learned helplessness is a mediator between racial discrimination and depressive symptoms for African American young adults. In other words, those who had depressive symptoms in their sample—approximately 37 percent—were also experiencing helplessness as a response to racial discrimination. For them, they would experience racial discrimination and feel helpless, triggering depression.

Many of us feel bone dry and empty—tired, exhausted, fatigued, frustrated, and ready to stop moving. I am an African American who keeps it moving in my life, trying to move toward my values. But it is still not without cost—the extra energy and time it takes to push upstream. No lie, getting it done is *hard*. It takes effort. So, this directly relates, in an inverse manner, to committed action. But first, we must have the heart to dream.

What Is Your Dream?

Ask yourself: have you given up on your dreams? Have you ever even dared to dream? Our ancestors did not deserve the systemic oppression they received through slavery and beyond, and neither do we. Although racism was prevalent, our ancestors did dare to dream. Harriet Tubman not only longed to be free but she also dreamed that thousands of others would be free as well. And she pushed toward that reality. Martin Luther King Jr. had a dream. "I still have a dream. It is a dream deeply rooted in the American dream."

What do you dream for yourself, for your loved ones? If you let go of your dream, will you pick it up again? We can acknowledge that systemic inequity makes things hard for us. We can recognize that our journey sometimes is rocky, tedious, and painful. But if we don't hold onto our dreams, values, and hope for a golden life, what do we have? You deserve to move toward your golden life. Through joy and pain, you deserve to move, step by step, toward living life like it's golden. Are you willing to pick yourself up, dust yourself off, and start moving toward what matters to you again? Committed action can help you begin.

Getting It Done Personally

There are some beautiful things about committed action, as defined in ACT, when applied to our values. "The process of committed action invites us to notice how we are responsible for our own actions" (Bennett & Oliver 2019). And indeed, we are responsible for our actions. However, when it comes to African Americans and other oppressed groups, we want to make sure that we do not simplify this. To just say,

"We are responsible for our actions" leans toward Eurocentric, WASP (White Anglo-Saxon Protestant) American thinking regarding our independence and ability to pull ourselves up by our bootstraps. While people are responsible for their own actions, sometimes systems affect people such that their efforts are hindered or affected in other ways. Thus, for you as an African American experiencing systemic inequity, you need to know: Yes, you are responsible for your own actions. Still, I also wholeheartedly acknowledge the impact of culture and how it may affect your struggle. So, before I help you take the values you identified in the last chapter and put them into action, let's acknowledge that you're tired. We are tired. Still, you deserve to attain something in your life that matters to you! You deserve it, and you are *worth* it.

So, to build on your values, what is one thing, no matter what size, that you can commit to today that would bring you closer to the qualities you want to be about?

Getting It Done Collectively

ACT does a great job of looking at our individual values and how we can commit to action toward them. For African Americans, though, we mustn't just move forward on individual values but also on collective values. In chapter seven, we discussed the values that we collectively hold due to systemic oppression. Some of these values include:

- reconnection to family, including extended family (it takes a village)

- communal unity, and collective work/responsibility

- communal freedom—economically and otherwise

- self-determination, collective voice, tenacity, and persistence

- collective faith, communal worship, belief in ourselves, and belief in our ultimate success

- collective purpose, restoration, creativity to benefit our communities

Because collaborative committed action work is so important for African Americans, I believe that we need to culturally tailor ACT to our need for collective action. I am not saying that personal work is not helpful. However, healing our anxiety, depression, or trauma can be more potent when we become a collective village for one another while healing. Also, complete healing cannot occur if we focus only on the individual pain we suffer (personal anxiety or trauma) while trauma is still happening to all of us on a systemic level. If we can learn how to collectively empower ourselves and create a village to tackle collective values that matter to us, we can successfully move toward greater levels of healing.

In research, there is a great deal of literature surrounding social supports and how having family, friends, or other people to turn to in good times and bad can significantly improve mental health outcomes. For instance, one article about a mental health approach to COVID-19 effects discussed a culturally specific mental health and spirituality approach for African Americans. They discussed the importance of creating social support spaces. They stated that one of the crucial aspects of their intervention was the emphasis on the "power and importance of relationships and trust in creating and maintaining collaboration, crafting the public health messages that are believable and trustworthy, and raising the probability of utilizing secular mental health services." (Thompkins Jr. et al. 2020, 456).

The concept behind "sister circles" or "brother circles" is not new; these concepts have been used for centuries in Black communities (Neal-Barnett et al. 2011). The idea of wellness circles or empowerment circles, however, goes beyond simply social support. These are groups of individuals that are actively working toward healing, both individually and collectively. There is no way to effect change on the political, economic, and other systems in America by ourselves alone. But if each of us can connect with a group, a village, or a multitude of like-minded persons, we collectively can effect change toward our collective values, no matter how large or small the change is. Thus, culturally tailored ACT can potentially be a powerful tool to help us heal and grow in psychological flexibility, both personally and collectively.

There are things that you have determined that you value for our culture—for your family and our communities. Now, this is where we come together collectively to "get it done." Gather your peers and colleagues; they are part of your village. And it takes a village to get it done collectively—*we cannot do this alone.*

Research shows that those who move, even in simple steps, toward improving their collective situation—whether through advocacy or standing up in small ways one minute at a time—end up being more empowered, more enlightened, less depressed, and less anxious. And they are contributing to making changes, no matter how small, in the world we live in and how things get done.

So, start brainstorming about ways, small or large, that you and your village can start living toward at least one of our collective values.

EXERCISE: Engaging in Collective, Communal Action

This exercise can and should be done with the same group that you engaged in collective values work with during the last chapter.

As a group, revisit the list of values that you collectively identified. Focus on those few values that most agreed were very important to address. The following script can be used to begin the discussion of how to actively move toward collective values:

> *"So, let's talk about the collective values work we did. We did not just do that as a useless exercise. These are things that you have determined that you value for our culture—for your families and for our communities. So, this is where we come together collectively. Those around you are now part of your village. And it takes a village to get it done collectively. We cannot do this alone."*

Research shows that those who move, even in simple steps, toward improving their collective situation, whether it is through advocacy or standing up in small ways one minute at a time end up being more empowered, more enlightened, less depressed, and less anxious. And they are contributing to making changes, no matter how small, in the world we live in and how things get done.

So, let's take today to collectively brainstorm about ways, small or large, that we can start living toward at least one of our collective values."

After reading the script, the group can begin to discuss small and larger ways to move toward values. Collective action may also include actions such as group advocacy. There are advocacy toolkits for those groups and "villages" who want to learn more together about how to make an impact.

Community Health Worker Advocacy Toolkit

http://peersforprogress.org/wp-content/uploads/2013/12/20131206_wg6_chw_advocacy_toolkit.pdf.

This toolkit assembles a set of resources (e.g., fact sheet, talking points, resources for digital advocacy, action steps, and case studies) that can be useful to change state and national policy.

The University of Kansas Community Tool Box: Using Social Media for Digital Advocacy

https://ctb.ku.edu/en/table-of-contents/advocacy/media-advocacy.

This resource introduces key steps and examples for using social media for digital advocacy.

Advocacy Toolkit: Skills and Strategies for Effective and Peer Advocacy

https://www.brainline.org/article/advocacy-toolkit-skills-and-strategies-effective-and-peer-advocacy.

This resource helps people in four ways: self-advocacy, peer advocacy, systems advocacy, and legal advocacy.

Using African Folklore to Get It Done

One of the intriguing things about ACT is its use of metaphors and interactional exercises. The use of metaphor is purposeful and powerful because the goal of ACT is to help us "circumvent some of the problems that are inherent in literal language by shifting away from traditional dialogue and moving toward a more experiential encounter" (Stoddard & Afari 2014, 2). Metaphors help us to understand on an experiential level rather than just an intellectual level.

African folklore, which has culturally been part of a storytelling tradition for us for generations, can help us understand on an experiential level. The following is a story about how we can move toward "getting it done" in our lives.

An Ethiopian Folktale: *Three Hairs of a Lion*

Segab's mother died when he was eleven years old.

His father married another woman, Bizunesh by name.

Segab did not like Bizunesh. But Bizunesh began to love the boy very much and tried to be a good mother to him.

She always made good breakfasts, dinners, and suppers. But he did not eat them. She bought him many good clothes. But he did not look at them.

She gave him new shoes. But he went to the river and threw the shoes into the water. When she spoke to him, he always ran away.

One day the poor woman said to Segab, "I always wanted to have a son and now I have you, Segab. I love you very much, my dear boy!"

But, Segab said angrily, "I am not your son. And you are not my mother. My mother is dead. I do not love you. I will never love you."

Bizunesh was very sorry and cried all night. In the morning, she decided to go to a wise old man. She told him about Segab, who did not love her.

The old man said, "I can help you. But first, you must bring me three hairs of a lion."

"But how can I do this? The lion will kill me," Bizunesh said.

The old man said, "I cannot answer your question. I need three hairs of a lion. Try to get them."

So Bizunesh went out to try to get the hairs. She went far, far away from her house and came to a place where a lion lived. The lion was very big and roared angrily. He was hungry.

Bizunesh was afraid of him and ran away quickly. But the next day she came back with some meat for the lion. She put the meat not far from him and ran away.

The lion saw the meat and went to it. He ate it all very quickly.

The next day she again brought some meat for the lion and put it a little nearer. And again, the lion ate it all up.

Every day, Bizunesh brought some meat for the lion and he soon understood that the woman was his friend. He was not angry and he did not roar. He was happy to see her.

And one day, Bizunesh came very near to the lion and gave him the meat from her hand. At the same time, she tore three hairs off his back.

The lion was not angry. Bizunesh ran to the old man and showed him the hairs.

"What must I do with them now?" she asked.

"Nothing," he answered. "But you know how to go near a lion, little by little, step by step. Do the same with Segab. And I am sure he will love you."

What kind of courage did Bizunesh show as she faced the lion? What kind of wisdom, patience, and tenacity? The old man said that if she showed these same attributes to Segab, "I am sure he will eventually love you."

What are the "Segabs" in your life? What are the values that you love that don't love you right now? Consider the work are you willing to put in to get your Segabs (your values) to work for you.

Stories, folklore, fables, and messages like these can be used as a talking point with your village. Through metaphors and culturally rich messages like these, we can begin to function as our African ancestors traditionally did before families were torn apart via slavery. Before slavery, families used to pass knowledge down from generation to generation through stories and fables. They used to talk, commune, and brainstorm together about what mattered to their communities. Through this collective brainstorming, we are better able to engage in committed action to address the systemic inequities that we face.

We can both identify our personal and collective values and attain them. We can live life like it is golden by moving toward our values one step, one action at a time. And we do not have to do this thing alone! In the next chapter, "Hexa-dancing with Blacks in America," we will define hexa-dancing and bring together everything you have learned in this book.

CHAPTER 9

Bringing It All Together: Hexa-dancing with Blacks in America

Father, give us courage to change what must be altered, serenity to accept what cannot be helped, and the insight to know the one from the other.

—Reinhold Niebuhr

I don't know if you have ever watched the Dance Theatre of Harlem perform. If you have not, it is such a treat! The Dance Theatre of Harlem is a professional ballet company and school based in Harlem, New York City, founded in 1969. It is known as the first Black classical ballet company and the first major ballet company to prioritize Black dancers.

As the dancers move, the only way I can describe it is that is ordered chaos. Sometimes, movements look random or are unexpected by the observer. But I can assure you that every move has been thought out and has a purpose or a meaning. Words cannot justify how beautiful it is to watch them.

I bring them up as an example because Steven Hayes has described using ACT as "a hexa-dance." Hexa-dancing is also ordered chaos. I am sure you may be wondering what hexa-dancing is. The root word of hexa-dancing is "hexa," meaning six (for the six core processes). In this book, I shared with you six things: "It Is What It Is," "In The Here and Now," "Freedom to Let Go," "I Am More Than My Experiences," "Living Life Like It's Golden," and "Getting It Done." These are called the six "core processes" in ACT, and ACT therapists use these to work with clients to help them move forward toward their values even amid pain.

Going through these processes is not like checking off tasks on a list. There is no specific sequential order in which you need to do these processes. For instance, you do not have to master defusion before moving to self-as-context or values. Instead, you do a kind of dance around these six processes. For instance, depending upon what was going on with you, you might start a bit with values or acceptance—or you might begin elsewhere. There is no rule about how long to engage each process since everyone is different. One person may need to address "It Is What It Is" for a more extended period, and another may struggle more with committed action ("Getting It Done"). So, what ends up happening is that you dance around these six processes, engaging the ones that most need attention at the time. When ACT is at its best, you will move back and forth among the core processes in a fluid, shifting, nonlinear way. All of the movement comes together with a purpose—to help you move toward your golden life.

So, the hexa-dance can be beautiful and purposeful. But I wanted to consider this hexa-dance for us as African Americans. What might influence how we dance?

Hexa-dancing: Can You Dance by Yourself?

I am sure that many of you have seen synchronized and choreographed dancing at some point. When two (or more) people are dancing and doing the exact same move at the exact same time, it is amazing! That is the type of interplay that a clinician and client can achieve in ACT therapy.

Of course, people can dance by themselves. There is also a beauty in free dance or the choreographed dance that a person does alone. Similarly, using some of the ACT tools alone without a therapist (such as reading books, doing workbooks, or engaging in exercises) can also be healing. You can receive something from a book like this without being in treatment. However, when it comes to hexa-dancing, the dance looks different with a therapist versus looking at the material alone. As an example, stories of two women are provided—one who engaged in hexa-dancing with a therapist, and the other going it alone.

Hexa-dancing Alone

Dawyna is an African American female nurse who has been in her present nursing position at a hospital for seven years. She has experienced many microaggressions and racial slights over the years by her primarily non-Black coworkers. But when a white woman with less experience was recently hired and then almost immediately elevated to a position above her, Dawyna got extremely upset.

Dawyna heard about ACT from one of her relatives. She began buying audiobooks about ACT and listening to them as she traveled to and from work. As she learned pieces of the hexaflex, she began to put them into action in her life in a kind of self-paced dance. She started off by examining her values, then moved swiftly to committed action (both personal and collective). She began to make bold steps and questioned her boss about why she has not yet been promoted. She also began to work on changing the system at her hospital so that it would more readily recruit and retain nurses of color.

Hexa-dancing in Therapy

Professor Bobette is a Black woman professor in the mathematics department of a university. It has been an uphill battle for her in academia since she started, given that most professors in math departments are male and non-Black. Bobette fought hard for years, always doing double the work of her peers. She made working nights and weekends a personal lifestyle, and she sacrificed lots of her time and her social life for her job. She thought the sacrifice was worth it because she was promoted from assistant professor to associate professor, and then much later to full professor.

Professor Bobette was fine with her job—until she accidentally became aware of the salary differences in the university. She realized that, as a full professor, she was barely making a few hundred dollars more than a recent assistant professor hire. Also, she discovered that her white male counterparts were making almost $10,000 more than her at the same academic level.

Professor Bobette became depressed. She heard about ACT through a friend and started seeking counseling. During her virtual counseling sessions, Bobette and her therapist danced around the hexaflex. They started off discussing self-as-context and defusion because of some of Professor Bobette's thoughts ("I am easily taken advantage of" and "There's nothing I can do to be validated or compensated well at my job"). They danced toward a discussion of her values, and bounced back and forth around the hexaflex until the came to committed action later on in treatment.

I want to make the point that this hexa-dance interplay between the six parts of the hexaflex works *best* in treatment with an ACT-practicing therapist. Although there is some beauty in working this dance on your own, it is much more effective and satisfying when interacting as a client in treatment with an ACT-trained coach or counselor.

It is known that some in the African American community think negatively about mental health therapy. It is well-documented that African Americans under-utilize mental health treatment, and that we at times will suffer silently and longer with an emotional issue than necessary. Mental health stigma is a big problem in the African American community, and in many cases rightfully so. Due to the Tuskegee experiments and the negative racist historical relationship psychology has had with Blacks, many are distrustful of the mental health system.

We also hear messages from our community members, friends, family, and churches that you have to be "crazy" to go to therapy.

It is possible that you have received messages in your life that have downplayed the usefulness of therapy. Or you may have been embarrassed, ashamed, or fearful of what your loved ones might think about you if you started therapy with someone. Although going to therapy is a choice and not mandatory to receive help from this book, I encourage you to attempt to free yourself of any cultural or other barriers that will keep you from getting the full and complete healing that you desire and deserve.

Knowing When It Is Internal or External

As African Americans, there are always personal issues that we can and should work on, and there are times when we should yield ourselves to do the work that needs to be done to make our lives more golden. For instance, what if someone who has a fear of elevators has just been offered his dream job—which just happens to be on the thirtieth floor of a high-rise building. It would behoove that individual to do some personal internal work to address that fear so that they could live their golden life and enjoy their dream job.

On the other hand, what if that same person did not fear elevators but instead was experiencing ongoing systemic racism at their "dream job" that was causing them undue stress. Possibly that person, despite the job being a "dream," is experiencing minimizations and racial slights weekly, and they may not feel as if they will be able to move up the corporate ladder any further than where they are because of their skin color. In this case, the person doesn't need to address a personal internal problem. Instead, they will need, somehow, to address a systemic, external problem—the problem of racial bias at their job. The stories of Dawyna and Professor Bobette both identified systemic, external problems that affected their personal well-being.

Blacks in America do not just have to address the internal issues that keep us from our golden lives; we also have to address the external problems that get in the way. In regard to these systemic, external problems, we may need to decide when to hold onto the cards we are dealt and fight, and when to walk away or fold.

This internal/external conflict is extremely important for us to consider. The evidence-based psychological healing tradition in America is primarily based on Eurocentric, Western values. Although some evidence-based interventions add Eastern-based philosophies like mindfulness into the mix, psychological models are still based primarily on either an individual's pathologies (the medical model) or an individual's strengths (recovery models). Either way, they are based more on the individual and less on the individual in context.

It is so important to avoid blaming ourselves as the victim—we cannot focus only on our personal internal struggles while ignoring systemic issues that affect us. Strategies for tackling individual issues may not be the same as strategies for tackling systemic issues. As African Americans, we need to learn when to hold onto certain thoughts and behaviors because they may be self-protective, when to release them, what battles to fight based upon our values, and what battles to refrain from fighting.

The quote at the beginning of this chapter is from Reinhold Niebuhr, the originator of the Serenity Prayer in the *Big Book of Alcoholics Anonymous* (*AA Big Book* 2002). The serenity prayer says, "God, grant me the serenity to accept the things I cannot change, the courage to change the things I can, and the wisdom to know the difference." As Blacks in America, we would benefit from this skill. As I shared in chapter 3, "It Is What It Is—Acceptance," for African Americans, there is a difference between accepting internal thoughts and feelings versus accepting the outcome of external systemic events. Understanding what should be accepted, what should be changed, and the differences between these two are vital for us.

Creative Hopelessness for African Americans

What is "creative hopelessness"? Creative hopelessness is an optional part of acceptance work (It Is What It Is) in the ACT model. Another way to describe it is "hitting bottom" or coming to the limits of yourself. "Hitting bottom" is a term used in Alcoholics Anonymous circles and other substance treatment circles. Hitting bottom is when you become fully aware of all of the things that you have tried and done to control your environment, and you realize that none of those things you tried have worked. Your methods of distraction have not worked to help your situation. Your other strategies such as using substances or self-harm have not worked. Your attempts to control your thinking have not worked. Your attempts to avoid or evade thinking about the problem have not worked. Hitting bottom means that you realized that everything you have tried has not worked. This puts you in a place of humility, to be willing to learn new ways of addressing the problem.

We talked about the struggle for control in chapter 3. There, we talked about how sometimes we get wrapped up, tied up, and tangled up, attempting to control our pain. We may try to control our pain by applying strength, willpower, or denial, self-medicating, or ignoring our thoughts and feelings while experiencing the pain. When it comes to our experience as African Americans facing ongoing systemic inequities or racism, sometimes those attempts at control are self-protective. For someone who is not in a safe situation—for instance, living in a violent area where your life may potentially be in danger because of the color of your skin—there is a constant need to be on guard, the need to self-protect or to protect loved ones. As I stated in chapter 3, the desire for control is even more prominent if you feel you do not have much external control.

Getting to a place of creative hopelessness can help us to be willing to allow our thoughts and feelings to be as they are in the moment, whether they are pleasant or painful, wanted or unwanted. But how does the process of creative hopelessness work for those of us who may still face real external dangers—those who are not entirely safe?

The answer lies in what we as Blacks are "hitting bottom" about. We can hit bottom when it comes to our own private internal processes (discussed earlier). That is, the way we think, the things we do, the ways we feel—everything tied to what is under our personal locus of control. However, we cannot "hit bottom" about external systemic issues because external systemic issues such as racism, discrimination, and inequities require a different, separate response. To demonstrate this, a creative hopelessness exercise for African Americans follows.

Hitting Bottom for Blacks

In this exercise (adapted from Russ Harris), you will choose an experience that you are struggling with. Answer the questions about your experience in the order that they are presented:

- Name the thoughts or experiences that you are struggling with. What thoughts, feelings, emotions, sensations, and urges do these thoughts or experiences bring up for you?

- Identify the nature of each experience (this is important). Is the experience within your personal control? Or, is this experience due to some systemic issue going on outside of yourself? Mark each thought or experience as either blue or red. Blue means that the thought is something that you probably have personal control over. Red means that it is something that happens outside of you, like a systemic issue. Systemic issues are things that might occur in government, politics, law, or some other setting that you do not personally control.

- Place the red thoughts or experiences (system or externally related) to the side. You are only working with the blue thoughts or experiences right now.

- *For the blue thoughts only*—what are some of the main ways you've tried to avoid or get rid of this thought or experience? List the ways you have attempted to avoid or get rid of it.

- *For the blue thoughts only*—Have you put a lot of time and effort and energy into getting rid of your thoughts or experiences? Have any of the methods you used given you long-term relief from the problem? Has anything you've tried permanently gotten rid of the problem? How long before the problem comes back again?

- *For the blue thoughts only*—What has it cost you, doing all these things to try to get rid of the problem? List your costs in terms of work, health, time, money, energy, relationships, missing out, or giving up on important things. Explore the long-term costs. Was all of the time and energy you spent worth it overall? You have tried so hard for so long. What's that like for you?

- *For the blue thoughts only*—What would you say to someone you love, if they had been caught in the same trap as you for so long, and they were feeling what you are feeling right now?

- *For the blue thoughts only*—What does hitting bottom look like for you? Do you feel you need to try more things to control your situation, or have you hit bottom? (If you have hit bottom) Are you willing to try something different in terms of building a better life?

As noted in the exercise, we are discussing hitting bottom for only the statements *clearly within our internal control*. We do not work in this way on the thoughts or experiences that are tied to systemic outside factors because doing so would blame the victim. For those things outside of our locus of control, we may instead engage in the type of empowering committed action that we discussed in the previous chapter.

Workability for African Americans

The question of workability is a big part of ACT. Workability asks the question: "Is it working for you? Is your avoidance working for you? Is your control working for you?"

For African Americans, this is not always a solid and clear "No, it's not working." Instead, someone like Dr. Bobette might answer, "Yes, kind of. It has worked for me to be able to survive [in academia], to continue to keep putting one foot in front of the other, to keep from just giving up altogether."

Thus, as a part of our healing work as African Americans, *we need and deserve validation*. We need to know and to be told that the avoidance and other defense behaviors that we used to navigate through severe pain or systemic trauma worked to help us survive. It is important for us to recognize that some of our defense mechanisms and avoidance behaviors worked for us to just keep moving. That struggle that we have gone through to survive should not be dismissed—it should be validated and seen as resilience. However, we do need to remember that there is a big difference between surviving and thriving. Some of us would like to stop merely existing. Instead, some of us would like to live life like it's golden. Just pulling through is completely different from living an abundant life, a life filled with things you value. The adaptive behaviors that we use to survive are not the same as those we will need to thrive. So, the workability question can be reworded slightly for African Americans, to increase its impact. Is it working for you to live your life like it is golden?

Adding to the Hexa-dance for African Americans

The beauty of ACT is that it is, by nature, flexible. It teaches us how to live a flexible life, and the process in and of itself is flexible and applicable to all human situations. In the case of African Americans, the dance can be enhanced if themes that are vital to us can be incorporated into the ACT process.

Movement toward Autonomy

A Chinese philosopher once said, "Give a man a fish, and you feed him for a day. Teach him how to fish, and you feed him for a lifetime." Despite stereotypes of us as lazy or desiring handouts, African Americans have longed to have our own since before slavery. There is an intense desire for equity—equal opportunity for self and family actualization. We want the American dream to be true for everyone—including African Americans. Thus, there is a desire to have the opportunities to advance or own businesses, buy and sell properties, educate ourselves and our children, etc. Not a handout, but a movement toward self-autonomy. Thus, the hexa-dance should also move us to a place where we can eventually move in psychological flexibility independently.

Voice

One of the things that we African Americans desperately desire is voice. Voice means being seen and heard. It means that when something is said, it is listened to, acted on, and taken to heart. Voice is what Keisha in the last chapter desperately desired when she stood before the judge in the courtroom. Voice is what George Floyd wanted, as did the Black witnesses of George Floyd's death, who were yelling and shouting at the police officer just to let him up. We have had little voice in politics, in the boardrooms where business deals occur, in academia. We live our lives with the threat of being silenced, at times to the point of death. For generations, our voice has been snuffed out through lynchings and other ways, often through violent and deadly means. "I am not heard" has become "I can't breathe,"—the last words of Eric Garner, an unarmed man who was killed in 2014 after being put in a chokehold by a New York City police officer.

Belonging has been described in the research literature as a basic human need. It is sad to say that some African American people have not experienced much belonging, given that our ancestors were snatched from where we belonged, and we have been misplaced in a land that does not claim us as its own. We may not be able to experience belonging, but a voice? At least, hopefully, we can have a say. We can feel heard and seen. In Africa, those speaking the Zulu language greet each other with "*Sawubona!*" Sawubona does not mean "hello"— it means "I see you." Sawubona recognizes the worth and the dignity of each person. We, as African Americans, want that so badly—just to be acknowledged, seen, and heard.

Relationship (Village)

Another critical desire of African Americans is relationship. This desire for relationship is cultural, passed down from generation to generation. In Africa, we functioned as communities rather than individuals, as extended family systems and villages compared with the competitive nature of the United States. The desire for relationship intensified when we were denied connection through slavery. Family after family was torn apart during those hundreds of years of slavery, but the desire for relationship never left us. Dr. Joy DeGruy, the author of *Post-Traumatic Slave Syndrome,* has stated that the primary method for healing us is relationship. Building a relationship and rapport with clients is often discussed in therapeutic circles, but connection is vital in general when working with African Americans. Because of our history, many of us may experience distrust in systems—distrust in therapists, distrust in mental health settings. That distrust was coined "cultural distrust" by Arthur Whaley. Suspicion is logical, based upon the number of harmful and discriminatory encounters some of our ancestors and us have had with various systems in the past. It may take longer or a bit more work to establish trust with an African American client—not all, of course, but some. Before divulging our information, it is essential for us to feel safe and protected in a relationship, including relationships with therapists. There should be authenticity and transparency present. Only after establishing that trust can real work begin. Thus, relationship is critical for African Americans.

In summary, there is a way that we can dance in the fire of the pain that we endure—that dance is called hexa-dancing. But the genre of dance that African Americans dance in and out of therapy may be slightly different from others who hexa-dance because we have different needs based on our unique history.

We will conclude our discussion in the next chapter, "In the Fire Yet Not Consumed."

CHAPTER 10

In the Fire, Yet Not Consumed

Keep being compassionate to those who still have doubts, and snatch others out of the fire to save them...

—Jude 1:22–23, *The Passion*

Fire can be helpful, or it can be all-consuming. For some people, the fire of situations in their life is painful but valuable. For others, the fire of their lives is consuming them, and they need a lifeline urgently.

Sometimes the fire of tribulation and trials in our lives are too much to bear alone. Occasionally, we may need a little help. Needing and reaching out for help is never wrong. In our culture, we have looked at counseling or seeking support for our problems as a weakness. It is well-known that there is much stigma attached to getting help for emotional problems in our culture as African Americans. There are so many reasons for this. Some are the beliefs and notions passed down from our forefathers to us, which could include:

- Mental illness is due to a person's sins.

- Someone who is having emotional breakdown/problems is weak. We are supposed to be strong Black men and women. We can't show weakness.

- Mental illness is not real. It is just another label the dominant culture gives to oppressed populations to keep them under their thumb.

- What happens in the family should stay in the family.

- You shouldn't take medication. It's harmful or ungodly (distrust it).

- It is not normal to talk to a stranger about your problems. If you pray and get closer to God, you can be healed.

- Your problem will go away by itself if you ride it out.

- Certain herbs and practices passed down through the generations will help you. Professional help is only a last resort after trying everything else.

- A good stiff drink or a good bag of weed will cure your problems (self-medication).

- You should go to a witch doctor, shaman, priest, pastor, rabbi, imam, or other spiritual leaders.

- There's nothing wrong with your mind; it's your body. You should go to a hospital, emergency room, or doctor.

Despite what we have learned, it is perfectly okay to seek outside help when things get "too hot." When the fire of tribulation and trials in your life moves from being contained to being overwhelming, nothing is wrong with seeking help. There is nothing wrong with you. If anything, you are taking care of yourself. You are seeking a hand out of the fire when the fire becomes too overwhelming.

There is no magic wand that can wave the pain away. It looks like systemic oppression, for example, is not going away any time soon. We may be roasted by the fire of racism, discrimination, or oppression in our life again. Also, there is no guarantee that a traumatic event won't occur in our lives in the future. However, there is a way to learn how to move through the fire of pain without being consumed. That way is through the use of ACT.

Throughout this book, I have attempted to be authentic and transparent about how ACT practices unfold in my life. I do this to share how the fires in life burn yet don't consume me—and often even refine me. During the many months that I was working on this book, several painful events happened. My husband of seventeen years died. I went through several severe family challenges that were so painful that I spent many nights in tears. During this time, certain loved ones and I received certain unfavorable and challenging medical diagnoses. COVID-19 affected all of us, but it affected my job in that they had to make budget cuts and salary reductions. And the second pandemic— the racism pandemic—affected me as I am sure it affected you.

In spite of everything that happened, I kept writing this book. There were times when I wanted to stop, times when I felt like giving up. There were moments when my old tapes would play. "You are not good enough to write a book." "You don't have anything significant to say." There were times when I felt so paralyzed that I did not think that

I could move. But I did move. I met every book deadline. If I had not been using the principles of ACT to move toward my values and what mattered to me, I never would have made it.

The values that guided me were my faith in my God, my passion for helping others, and my desire to impact Black lives with this book. Using ACT helped me to move forward toward my values, in spite of the pain I was in. Through ACT, I learned, day by day, how to stay in the present moment rather than anxiously looking too far into the future. I engaged in more meditative practices during a time when the world really needed more peace and tranquility. I started seeing myself as more than my past experiences, more than my education or achievements, more than even my religion. I started separating myself from old tapes and thoughts such as "I am not good enough." I became much more "woke," and I began to clearly recognize the state of my existence and the existence of those around me. I also gave up my prior avoidance behaviors. For instance, I used to use food to comfort me, even though that was opposite to my value of good health. So, I use food for comfort less and less, and I face my circumstances more and more.

As a result, I noticed a really wonderful thing: I started taking many more risks in life. I risked writing this book. I risked trying for a job I would have never tried for in the past, and I got the job. I risked moving cross-country to the job, leaving my family and friends, and I love the new place that I live. I began risking saying yes more and more to activities that I would have said no to before because of feeling like an impostor. Now I can say that I am closer to living my life like it's golden. I am not there yet, but I am closer. Do painful things still happen? Of course. But I am closer to my golden life than I was before, and there is some peace and joy in that.

POOF is ACT applied to the Black American experience. We can, in our pain, get to a place where we realize "It Is What It Is" and we have "Freedom to Let Go," recognize that we are "More Than Our Experiences" and begin living "In the Here and Now," then map out for ourselves what it would be like to "Live Life Like Its Golden," and we can "Get It Done." This is how we arrive at a place where we can begin to dance in our fire.

This is how the POOF (Pulling Out Of Fire) model can enable us to move forward in our lives toward our values, despite the pain. And it can also help us empower ourselves to create sister and brother circles and communities that can change the systemic injustice we continuously face.

Stephanie's Story

Stephanie smiled as she sat on her front porch of her apartment, reflecting. She cannot believe how things changed so drastically for her in a year. She thought back on this time last year at Thanksgiving. Last year, she felt that she had nothing to be thankful for. She was actually hopeless and suicidal this time last year, wondering why she was even alive.

She had so many losses last year. Her favorite aunt and her close friend of over fifteen years had both died of chronic health conditions. Her divorce was finalized two years ago, and she became the single parent of two elementary-school-aged children. Due to the economic downturn, her job laid off workers, and she was one of those laid off. She remembered the scramble she had last year as she tried to make financial ends meet for her family even while her children were at home because she could not afford daycare. And she remembered all of the strain and pressure she felt in her neighborhood over the past year or two. She lives and was raised in a neighborhood that has high levels of police racial profiling and death-by-cop percentages for Black males. She remembers the fear she had for her own eleven-year-old son Andre's welfare every time he walked to school—a fear that has not completely left her. Last year at this time, Stephanie was ready to give up fighting. She was bone-tired.

But she was introduced to a friend who told her about ACT. Stephanie started researching ACT on the internet, and she began to read books and articles about it. She contacted an agency that provided free counseling to Black women, and she started counseling with someone at the agency. Stephanie started to use some self-help tools such as mindfulness apps and a free ACT app she obtained. Stephanie has even been motivated toward actions based on her personal and communal values ("getting it done"). She has become more involved in her community and has joined an organization of other Black mothers who want to protect their Black sons and daughters from police violence and racism.

Through her year-long journey toward greater self-understanding and healing, Stephanie knows now that she has grown so much. Many of the situations in her life have not changed. She is still a single parent, she still has grief about losing dear ones, and she still has some fear about the systemic racism in her city and how it may impact her children. But her perspective has changed. She knows what matters to her and she's making steps toward those things that matter. And she does not feel alone in the fight anymore.

Stephanie has not smiled for a long time. But this Thanksgiving, she is sure that there will be a smile or two coming from her as they sit around the dinner table.

As we have been discussing throughout this book, ACT has the goal of helping us improve our psychological flexibility: the ability to live and breathe in the fire moments of our lives and dance in the fire. We have looked at these elements from an African American perspective, and thus, the culturally tailored POOF model.

I am not going to idolize ACT or put it on a pedestal. It is not magic. But it has been a tool that has helped many move toward what matters to them, and it can help you too. Systemic inequities will not miraculously change any time soon. But being aware and "woke," staying in the present, being free from the handcuffs of the mind— these things will help us to be freer to move closer toward both our individual and collective values as Black people. And when our minds are free, we will be better able to effect change together on both individual and systemic levels.

Refined in Fire

While pain in our life is inevitable, it does not have to overwhelm us or derail our lives. We can either be burned to ashes in the fire of our pain and despair, or we can allow the fire of pain to refine us.

What does it mean to be refined? Of course, everyone is not spiritual or religious. But African Americans have such a rich historical tradition of using faith as a protective factor and support during hard times. Culturally, our ancestors throughout the generations have sought solace through their faith. Thus, we can look at a spiritual source—the Bible—for some clues on what it means to be refined in fire. Psalm 66:10–12 states:

> For you, God, tested us; you *refined us like silver.*
>
> You brought us into prison and laid burdens on our backs.
>
> You let people ride over our heads; we went through fire and water,
>
> but you brought us to a place of abundance.

To be "refined" means to be purified and to be free from things that are undesirable. ACT is a tool that can help you move toward a way of thinking that can cause you to be present in fire, yet not be consumed. It can help in your refining process, to help shed you of undesirable elements (like avoidance thoughts and behaviors). Once you are not seeking to cure or control your pain, no longer pretending that your pain will go away magically, you can use ACT. It will help you to acquire effective behavior patterns that will help change your perceptions and experiences of the pain.

You can be in pain but not struggle with the pain. You can be in pain but not avoid or self-medicate the pain. You can be in pain but not be consumed by the pain. Instead, as I did while writing this book, you can move toward your golden life and live it—even during pain. To do so is to use the fire to learn and grow. Rather than being consumed, you will emerge refined, like a phoenix out of the flames.

Building a Life That's Golden

The words of Angela Davis set the tone for the journey found in *Out of the Fire*: "We have to talk about liberating minds as well as liberating society." Coming to terms with the long-term effects of inequity in our social systems and our mental health structures, research, and approaches is beyond overdue. It is time to see what it means to be human in all persons, recognizing each with dignity, respect, and parity—acknowledging that each individual carries their own measure of joy and pain and that each individual deserves liberation, fulfilling their own desire to live a meaningful life. Yet, as inequity persists, more time passes where the pain carried by some is altered such that each day is beset with uncertainty. "Will I be accepted?" "Will I be safe?" "Will I be seen as human, as equal?" "Will I be able to move freely in my life?"

The freedom to move in the world unfettered from the burden of racial trauma, racial injustice, and structural racism is crucial in changing the disparities in mental health diagnoses and the mental health treatment experienced by African Americans. In *Out of the Fire: Healing Black Trauma Caused by Systemic Racism Using Acceptance and Commitment Therapy*, Dr. Jennifer Payne invites us to expand the context of our thinking, using ACT, reaching those who suffer inequities without holding them responsible in inappropriate ways, and leaning into the efforts to make essential changes in how to approach mental health in an open and full-hearted way. A part of this process involves taking a hard look at how we approach what it means to be mentally healthy.

Mental health, often defined as the absence of symptoms, limits our understanding of what it means to be human. The medical model will not suffice. Mental health includes a much more expansive quality of what it means to be alive. It includes the ability to feel fulfilled, the ability to love and play, to learn and grow, and to be free and exercise choice in your life. Perhaps it is time for society, mental health professionals, and psychology researchers to reconsider their approach to what is considered disordered. In reflecting on the current mental health diagnostic system, I have spent time mulling over its roots and initial developers. The diagnostic manual used in mental health treatment was first published in the 1950s and was written entirely by white males. In more recent iterations of the manual, women and persons of color have been more involved, but the tracks for what it means to have a mental disorder had already long been laid. This knowledge has given me pause. What does this mean for those who suffer long-standing trauma and injustices? What does this mean for those who carry the burden of generations of oppression? I worry it means that responses to this kind of world, reasonable responses of pain and fear, will once again fall prey to a system that holds a person's internal experience as the indicator of disease and disorder.

I write this not to dismiss biology, physiology, or other factors that can play a role in our internal experience. Nor do I write it to reject the quite real and often challenging internally felt experiences that lead us to seek help. Instead, I write it to invite deep and sincere reflection on our understanding of how people come to behave and experience in ways that land them inside of stigmatized categories referred to as disorders. Sadness, anxiety, and bodily symptoms are significantly related to race-based trauma, stressors, and other adverse life experiences. These are reasonable responses to environmental events. Yet, what is happening inside us is still held out as a critical mental health forerunner for holding people as broken or damaged.

Nonetheless, it is worth understanding what is affecting mental health on the outside of our skin. Rather than simply assuming that something is wrong or disordered on the inside, it is time to consider a more helpful understanding of emotional experiences among African Americans and other persons of color. It is time to consider that problems arise in the dynamic interaction of people, their learning history, and their environments. Maybe it's not just how they feel, think, and sense.

Assessing the circumstances of life and the context of the Black experience is a critical factor in determining well-being. Risk factors for mental health difficulties include socioeconomic disadvantage, income inequality, racial injustices, subordinate social status, ongoing racial trauma, and for many Black women, unremitting responsibility for the care of others, to name a few. Suppose you are unsure about this call to consideration. In that case, it may be helpful to reflect upon your level of environmental stress, age-old external factors, and other life circumstances that have led you to feel discomfort, pain, and fear in life. Perhaps allowing room for your circumstances while recognizing these likely natural responses to such conditions would allow for compassion—shying away from notions that you are disordered or broken—but simply human. And then magnify these stressors, factors, and circumstances by one hundred or a thousand. It is here that perhaps we can appreciate the role of protracted racial trauma and injustices that lead to suffering; even greater compassion and understanding are needed here as well as a full recognition of the human beings who have suffered these events.

In addition to expanding our understanding of what it means to be human, we have another barrier to surmount: satisfaction in life, positive emotions and thoughts, and the fulfillment of basic needs for belonging, competence, and autonomy have been traditionally viewed as the cornerstones of psychological health. However, these fail to depict the vacillating and conflicting forces that are revealed when trying to navigate the world. Providing the foundation for dignity, respect, equality, health, and well-being will mean reaching beyond the traditional, listening to those whose voices have been undervalued, hearing the pain of inequity, and working to support what's needed. It will take courage to let go of old ideas of eliminating pain and what it means to be human, and instead reach for meaning. It requires grit and flexibility to assist those who wish to rise into their sense of a fulfilling life not marred by inequities but instead linked to personal values. Dr. Payne leads the way for these possibilities in *Out of the Fire*.

In this book, Dr. Payne is assisting persons in America of African heritage to create meaning in a way that allows for the whole human experience to be acknowledged, understood, and acted upon. From sharing her poem in the first pages to writing about her personal experiences and adapting ACT to be culturally connected to the African American experience, she steps away from simply labeling the pain of her fellow ancestry as disordered without regard for history and context. By bringing ACT to life for the African American, Dr. Payne is leaning into a future where meaning and values guide the work done in living well. No longer is psychological help simply about diagnoses and the so-called symptoms of living unwell. It is now about opening to experience, being present and aware amid a life that contains pain and joy, and standing inside of resilience guided by values in creating a life that's golden.

—Robyn D. Walser, PhD
Coauthor of seven books on acceptance
and commitment therapy, including
The Heart of ACT

Acknowledgments

I am grateful for every person who has influenced my development. They helped shape me into who I am today and contributed to my ability to write this book. I thank my children, Jazmon and Brielle, for the privilege of being their mom—I have learned so much from them.

I am also grateful for the influence of those who have passed on to the other side of life. My mother was such a positive influence and always encouraged me every step of the way. She was the impetus for my artistic side. My father was a rock of stability in my life and fed the logical side of who I have become.

I thank Bishop Robert T. Douglas Sr. for his past influence in my life. Years ago, when the idea of POOF sprouted, I had only a title but no understanding of how it would develop. Bishop Douglas always encouraged vision, and I will be forever grateful for that. I also am thankful for the opportunity to mature with my spiritual sisters, Karen Allen and Lois LeBlanc.

I have a substantial "village" that has influenced me. I thank you to all of the colleagues I have met, collaborated with, cried, and laughed with along the way. Thank you to MEND (Carynne Williams, the board of directors, and the clinicians of color who collectively strive to mend oppressed communities).

To the ACT community—I say thank you. I am particularly grateful for ACT experts such as Meg McKelvie, Miranda Morris, Robyn Walser, Debbie Sorensen, and the other ACT for MEND trainers. I have learned so much from them. I thank Steven Hayes and the other founders of ACT for this beneficial process-based approach to human suffering.

Finally, I thank New Harbinger and PRAXIS for taking a chance on me. Thank you to the New Harbinger editors Georgia Kolias and Jennifer Holder, and thank you, Spencer Smith of PRAXIS, for your vision.

The POOF (Pulling Out Of Fire) Model

There is a scripture in the Bible—Jude 22–23—that states, "Be merciful to those who doubt; save others by snatching them from the fire; to others show mercy, mixed with fear—hating even the clothing stained by corrupted flesh" (New International Version). The name POOF or Pulling Out Of Fire is influenced by this scripture. Some people simply need a little mercy and compassion to move forward from living a life where they are wandering and lost. But others need more. They may need a more urgent, interactive helping hand to pull out the fire toward healing and restoration. It becomes clear that mercy is a good start for that second group, but mercy and compassion are *not enough*. For that second group, it becomes clear that our mercy must not negate or ignore the seriousness of the situation because the stakes are high for them. The use of the word "snatch" is an indicator of the urgency of the problem.

As we have been discussing throughout this book, ACT has the goal of helping us improve our psychological flexibility, the ability to live and breathe in the fire moments of our lives, and dance in the fire. The problems of psychological inflexibility (avoidance and other behaviors or thoughts that keep us stuck) look like this according to the POOF model:

ACT Inhexaflex: Staying Stuck

Time Hopping (Past and Future)

On The Run
(Experiential
Avoidance)

Living Like I'm Lost
(Lack of Values)

PSYCHOLOGICAL
INFLEXIBILITY

Wrapped Up, Tied Up,
and Tangled Up
(Cognitive Fusion)

Bone Dry and On
Empty (Inaction or
Unworkable Action)

Damaged Goods: I am what I have been through
(Attachment to the Conceptualized Self)

We have looked at these elements from an African American perspective, and thus the culturally tailored ACT model looks like this:

ACT Hexaflex: POOF Healing

In the Here and Now (Present-Moment Awareness)

It Is What It Is
(Acceptance)

Living Life Like It's
Golden (Values)

PSYCHOLOGICAL
FLEXIBILITY

Freedom to Let Go
(Cognitive Defusion)

Getting It Done
(Committed Action)

I Am More Than My Experiences (Self As Context)

POOF is ACT applied to the Black American experience. This POOF (Pulling Out Of Fire) model can enable us to move forward in our lives toward our values, despite the pain. But it can also help us empower ourselves to create sister and brother circles and communities that can change the systemic injustice we continuously face. For more information about the model, go to www.poof-pullingoutoffire.com.

Collective Committed Action Resources

It takes a village to address African American systemic change. When you are ready to move on your, your family's, or your community's collective values toward committed systemic action, you do not have to do it alone. Here are some organizations that are already fighting the fight. If you value what they value, feel free to join them. The list is not exhaustive, so do your research as well!

Advancement Project

https://advancementproject.org/about-advancement-project/

African American Advocacy Center for Persons with Disabilities

https://blackdisabilitycenter.org/what-we-do/

Black Lives Matter

https://blacklivesmatter.com/

Campaign Zero

https://campaignzero.org/

Color of Change

https://colorofchange.org/about/

Communities United Against Police Brutality

https://www.cuapb.org/

Fair Fight

https://fairfight.com/

Know Your Rights Camp

https://www.knowyourrightscamp.com/

National Association for the Advancement of Colored People (NAACP)

https://naacp.org/

National Alliance on Mental Illness (NAMI) for Blacks

https://nami.org/Your-Journey/Identity-and-Cultural-Dimensions/Black-African-American

No New Jails NYC

https://www.nonewjails.nyc/background

Reclaim the Block

https://www.reclaimtheblock.org/

The Bail Project

https://bailproject.org/

The Center for Black Health and Equity

https://centerforblackhealth.org/

The National Black Justice Coalition

https://nbjc.org/

Ujima Community (The National Center on Violence Against Women in the Black Community)

https://ujimacommunity.org/what-we-do/

Unicorn Riot

https://unicornriot.ninja/

For a clinician's guide to applying
the principles found in *Out of the Fire*,
visit http://www.newharbinger.com/49883.

References

A-Tjak, J. G. L., Davis, M. L., Morina, N., Powers, M. B., Smits, J. A. J., and Emmelkamp, P. M. G. "A Meta-Analysis of the Efficacy of Acceptance and Commitment Therapy for Clinically Relevant Mental and Physical Health Problems." *Psychotherapy and Psychosomatics* 84, no. 30 (2015): 30–36.

Alcoholics Anonymous Big Book (2002). New York: Alcoholics Anonymous World Services.

Alim, T. N., Feder, A., Graves, R. E., Wang, Y., Weaver, J., Westphal, M., and Charney, D. S. (2008). Trauma, Resilience, and Recovery in a High-Risk African-American Population. *American Journal of Psychiatry* 165, no. 12: 1566-1575.

Anderson, L. A. (2019). "Rethinking Resilience Theory in African American Families: Fostering Positive Adaptations and Transformative Social Justice." *Journal of Family Theory & Review* 11, no. 3: 385–397.

American Psychiatric Association. (2013). *Diagnostic and Statistical Manual of Mental Disorders.* https://doi.org/10.1176/appi.books.9780890425596.

Arthritis Foundation (2021). "Fibromyalgia." Accessed at https://www.arthritis.org/diseases/fibromyalgia.

Bennett, R. and Oliver, J.E. (2019). *Acceptance and Commitment Therapy: 100 Key Points and Techniques.* London: Routledge.

Brodsky, A. E. (1999). "'Making It': The Components and Process of Resilience Among Urban, African-American, Single Mothers." *American Journal of Orthopsychiatry* 69, no. 2: 148–160.

Broman, C. L., Mavaddat, R., and Hsu, S.-Y. (2000). "The Experience and Consequences of Perceived Racial Discrimination: A Study of African Americans." *Journal of Black Psychology* 26, no. 2: 165–180.

Brown, D. L. (2008). "African American Resiliency: Examining Racial Socialization and Social Support as Protective Factors." *Journal of Black Psychology* 34, no. 1: 32–48.

Brunjes G. B. (2010). "Spiritual Pain and Suffering." *Asian Pacific Journal of Cancer Prevention* (11 Suppl 1): 31–36.

Campbell, C. M., and Edwards, R. R. (2012). "Ethnic Differences in Pain and Pain Management." *Pain Management* 2, no. 3: 219–230. https://doi:10.2217/pmt.12.7.

Carson, E. A. (2020). "Prisoners in 2019 (October 2020, NCJ 255115)." *U. S. Department of Justice Office of Justice Programs Bureau of Justice Statistics*. Accessed at https://www.bjs.gov/content/pub/pdf/p19.pdf.

Castro, F. G., Barrera Jr, M., and Holleran Steiker, L. K. (2010). "Issues and Challenges in the Design of Culturally Adapted Evidence-Based Interventions." *Annual Review of Clinical Psychology* 6: 213–239.

CDC. (2018). "Centers for Disease Control and Prevention, Social Determinants of Health." Accessed at https://www.cdc.gov/social determinants/index.htm.

Center for American Progress (2020). "Systematic Inequality: How America's Structural Racism Helped Create the Black-White Wealth Gap." Accessed at https://www.americanprogress.org/issues/race/reports/2018/02/21/447051/systematic-inequality/.

Cherry, K. (2020). "Martin Seligman Biography: The Father of Modern Positive Psychology." Accessed at https://www.verywellmind.com/martin-seligman-biography-2795527.

Degruy Leary, J., and Robinson, R. (2005). *Post Traumatic Slave Syndrome: America's Legacy of Enduring Injury and Healing*. Milwaukie, OR: Uptone Press.

Degruy-Leary, J. (2017). *Post-Traumatic Slave Syndrome: America's Legacy of Enduring Injury*. Portland, OR: Joy Degruy Publications Inc.

Faison Sr., J.R. (2020) "A Letter to White People: Black Americans Are Exhausted." *Tennessean*, June 24, 2020, https://www.tennessean.com/story/opinion/2020/06/24/letter-white-people-black-americans-exhausted/3247279001/.

Follette, V., and Pistorello, J. (2007). *Finding Life Beyond Trauma: Using Acceptance and Commitment Therapy to Heal from Post-Traumatic Stress and Trauma-Related Problems*. Oakland, CA: New Harbinger Publications.

Gal, S.; Kiersz, A.; Mark, M.; Su, R., and Ward, M. (2020). "26 Simple Charts to Show Friends and Family Who Aren't Convinced Racism Is Still a Problem in America." *Business Insider*, July 8, 2020, https://www.businessinsider.com/us-systemic-racism-in-charts-graphs-data-2020-6#the-employment-population-ratio-measures-the-share-of-a-demographic-group-that-has-a-job-and-its-been-lower-for-black-people-for-years-1.

Gallon, K. & Seals, T. (2020). "For Centuries Black leaders Raised Voices for Justice: From Harriet Tubman To John Lewis, They Called for Change." *AARP Newsletter*, 10/7/2020. Accessed at https://www.aarp.org/politics-society/history/info-2020/quotes-racial-justice.html.

Garg S., Kim L, Whitaker M. (2020). "Hospitalization Rates and Characteristics of Patients Hospitalized with Laboratory-Confirmed Coronavirus

Disease." MMWR—*Morbidity Mortality Weekly Report* 2020 69, no. 14 (March 1–30, 2020), 458–464. http://dx.doi.org/10.15585/mmwr.mm6915 e3external icon.

Glaude, E.S. (2020). "James Baldwin Insisted We Tell the Truth About This Country. The Truth Is, We've Been Here Before." *Time*, June 25, 2020, https://time.com/5859214/james-baldwin-racism/.

Goodtherapy Staff (2018). "When Loss Hurts: 6 Physical Effects of Grief." May 20, 2018, https://www.goodtherapy.org/blog/when-loss-hurts-6 -physical-effects-of-grief-0520187.

Gordon, T., Borushok, J., and Polk, K. L. (2017). *The ACT Approach: A Comprehensive Guide for Acceptance and Commitment Therapy*. Eau Claire, WI: PESI Publishing & Media.

Hacker, T., Stone, P., and Macbeth, A. (2016). "Acceptance and Commitment Therapy—Do We Know Enough? Cumulative and Sequential Meta-Analyses of Randomized Controlled Trials." *Journal of Affective Disorders* 190: 551–565.

Hanks, A, Solomon, D., and Weller, C.E. (2018). Systemic Inequality: "How America's Structural Racism Helped Create the Black-White Wealth Gap." *Center for American Progress*, February 21, 2018, https://www.americanprogress.org/issues/race/reports/2018/02/21 /447051/systematic-inequality/.

Harris, R. (2008). *The Happiness Trap: How to Stop Struggling and Start Living: A Guide to ACT*. Boston: Trumpeter Books.

Harris, R. (2019). ACT *Made Simple: An Easy-to-Read Primer on Acceptance and Commitment Therapy*. Oakland, CA: New Harbinger Publications.

Harris, T. (2021). "How Fire Works." In *How Stuff Works, Geophysics*. Accessed at https://science.howstuffworks.com/environmental/earth /geophysics/fire1.html.

Harvard Medical School. (2010). "The Pain-Anxiety-Depression Connection." *Harvard Health Publishing*, August 3, 20201, https://www .health.harvard.edu/healthbeat/the-pain-anxiety-depression-connection.

Hayes, S. C., Strosahl, K. D., Bunting, K., Twohig, M., and Wilson, K. G. (2004). "What Is Acceptance and Commitment Therapy?" In *A Practical Guide to Acceptance and Commitment Therapy*, edited by Hayes, S.C., Strosahl, K.D., 3–29. Boston: Springer.

Hayes, S. C. (2005). *Get Out of Your Mind and Into Your Life: The New Acceptance and Commitment Therapy*. Oakland, CA: New Harbinger Publications.

Hayes, S. C., Strosahl, K. D., and Wilson, K. G. (2012). *Acceptance and Commitment Therapy: The Process and Practice of Mindful Change*. New York: Guilford Press.

Hayes, S. C. (2020). *A Liberated Mind: How to Pivot Toward What Matters.* New York: Penguin.

Heath, E. (2020). "Adaptability May Be Your Most Essential Skill in the COVID-19 World." *The Washington Post*, May 26, 2020, https://www.washingtonpost.com/lifestyle/wellness/adaptability-coronavirus-skills/2020/05/26/8bd17522-9c4b-11ea-ad09-8da7ec214672_story.html.

Jones, E., Huey, S. J., and Rubenson, M. (2018). "Cultural Competence in Therapy with African Americans." In *Cultural Competence in Applied Psychology*, edited by Frisby, C., and O'Donohue, W., 557–573: Boston: Springer.

Jones, J. M. (2007). "Exposure to Chronic Community Violence: Resilience in African American Children." *Journal of Black Psychology* 33, no. 2: 125–149.

Lin, L., Stamm, K., and Christidis, P. (2018). "How Diverse Is the Psychology Workforce?" *APA's Center for Workforce Studies, Monitor on Psychology* 49, no. 2: 19. Retrieved from https://www.apa.org/monitor/2018/02/datapoint.

Madubata, I. J., Odafe, M. O., Talavera, D. C., Hong, J. H., and Walker, R. L. (2018). "Helplessness Mediates Racial Discrimination and Depression for African American Young Adults." *Journal of Black Psychology* 44, no. 7: 626–643.

Moran, D. J. (2015). "Acceptance and Commitment Training in the Workplace." *Current Opinion in Psychology* 2: 26–31.

Mulvaney-Day, N. E., Earl, T. R., Diaz-Linhart, Y., and Alegría, M. (2011). "Preferences for Relational Style with Mental Health Clinicians: A Qualitative Comparison of African American, Latino and Non-Latino White Patients." *Journal of Clinical Psychology* 67m no. 1: 31–44.

NAMI. (2020). "Black/African American." Accessed at https://www.nami.org/your-journey/identity-and-cultural-dimensions/black-african-american.

Neal-Barnett, A., Stadulis, R., Murray, M., Payne, M. R., Thomas, A., and Salley, B. B. (2011). "Sister Circles as A Culturally Relevant Intervention for Anxious Black Women." *Clinical Psychology: Science and Practice* 18, no. 3: 266.

NPR. (2020). "Being Black in America: 'We Have A Place in This World Too'" Accessed at https://www.npr.org/2020/06/05/867060621/being-black-in-america-we-have-a-place-in-this-world-too.

NIDA—National Institute on Drug Abuse (March 11, 2021). "Opioid Overdose Crisis." Accessed at https://www.drugabuse.gov/drug-topics/opioids/opioid-overdose-crisis.

Oldster, K. J. (2016). *Dead Toad Scrolls*. Bradenton, Florida: Bookerlocker. Com Inc.

Öst, L.-G. (2014). "The Efficacy of Acceptance and Commitment Therapy: An Updated Systematic Review and Meta-Analysis." *Behaviour Research and Therapy* 61: 105–121.

Payne, J.S. (2020). "George Floyd's Curb Is My Curb Too." *The Faculty, Medium*, June 15, 2020, https://medium.com/the-faculty/george-floyds -curb-is-my-curb-too-ba4664527f82.

Payne, J. S. (2014). "Social Determinants Affecting Major Depressive Disorder: Diagnostic Accuracy for African American Men." *Best Practices in Mental Health* 10, no. 2: 78–95.

Reno, J. (2021). "Chronic Pain: The Impact On The 50 Million Americans Who Have It." *Healthline Health News*, https://www.healthline.com /health-news/chronic-pain-the-impact-on-the-50-million-americans -who-have-it.

Recovery Research Institute. (2020). "Acceptance and Commitment Therapy (ACT)." Accessed at https://www.recoveryanswers.org /resource/acceptance-commitment-therapy-act/.

Rothman, L. (2015, April 16). "Why MLK Was Jailed in Birmingham." *TIME*, https://time.com/3773914/mlk-birmingham-jail/.

Seligman, M. E. (1972). "Learned Helplessness. *Annual Review of Medicine* 23 (1), 407–412.

Shipp, E. R. (2019). "1619: 400 Years Ago, A Ship Arrived in Virginia, Bearing Human Cargo." *USA Today*. https://www.usatoday.com /story/news/investigations/2019/02/08/1619-african-arrival-virginia / 2740468002/.

Shim, R.S., Koplan, C., Langheim, F.J., Manseau, M.W., Powers, R.A., and Compton, M.T. (2014). "The Social Determinants of Mental Health: An Overview and Call to Action." *Psychiatric Annals* 44, 22–26.

Smout, M. F., Hayes, L., Atkins, P. W., Klausen, J., and Duguid, J. E. (2012). "The Empirically Supported Status of Acceptance and Commitment Therapy: An Update." *Clinical Psychologist* 16, no. 3: 97–109.

Solar O, Irwin A. (2010). "World Health Organization: A Conceptual Framework for Action on the Social Determinants of Health. Social Determinants of Health Discussion Paper 2 (Policy and Practice)." Accessed at https://apps.who.int/iris/bitstream/ handle/10665/44489/?sequence=1.

Swain, J., Hancock, K., Hainsworth, C., and Bowman, J. (2013). "Acceptance and Commitment Therapy in The Treatment of Anxiety: A Systematic Review." *Clinical Psychology Review* 33, no. 8: 965–978.

Smith, W. A., Allen, W. R., and Danley, L. L. (2007). "'Assume the Position...You Fit the Description' Psychosocial Experiences and Racial Battle Fatigue Among African American Male College Students." *American Behavioral Scientist* 51, no. 4: 551–578.

Stoddard, J. A., and Afari, N. (2014). *The Big Book of ACT Metaphors: A Practitioner's Guide to Experiential Exercises and Metaphors in Acceptance and Commitment Therapy*. Oakland, CA: New Harbinger Publications.

Twohig, M. P., and Levin, M. E. (2017). "Acceptance and Commitment Therapy as A Treatment for Anxiety and Depression: A Review." *Psychiatric Clinics* 40, no. 4: 751–770.

Twelve Steps and Twelve Traditions. (1989). New York: Alcoholics Anonymous World Services.

Thompkins Jr, F., Goldblum, P., Lai, T., Hansell, T., Barclay, A., and Brown, L. M. (2020). "A Culturally Specific Mental Health and Spirituality Approach for African Americans Facing the COVID-19 Pandemic." *Psychological Trauma: Theory, Research, Practice, and Policy* 12, no. 5: 455.

Vujovich, M. (2014). "Understanding Spiritual Pain." *OSF Healthcare*. Accessed at https://www.osfhealthcare.org/blog/ understanding-spiritual-pain/.

Walker, R. (2020). *The Unapologetic Guide to Black Mental Health: Navigate an Unequal System, Learn Tools for Emotional Wellness, and Get the Help You Deserve*. Oakland, CA: New Harbinger Publications.

Walser, R. D., and Westrup, D. (2007). *Acceptance and Commitment Therapy for the Treatment of Post-Traumatic Stress Disorder and Trauma-Related Problems: A Practitioner's Guide to Using Mindfulness and Acceptance Strategies*. Oakland, CA: New Harbinger Publications.

Whaley, A. L. (2001). "Cultural Mistrust: An Important Psychological Construct for Diagnosis and Treatment of African Americans." *Professional Psychology: Research and Practice* 32, no. 6: 555.

Wilson, J. P., Hugenberg, K., and Rule, N. O. (2017). "Racial Bias in Judgments of Physical Size and Formidability: From Size to Threat." *Journal of Personality and Social Psychology* 113, no. 1: 59.

Yasharoff, H. (2019). "Justin Bieber Opens Up About 'Terrible Decisions', Being 'Disrespectful to Women." *USA Today*, September 3, 2019, https://www.usatoday.com/story/entertainment/celebrities/2019/09 /03/justin-bieber-talks-mental-health-struggles-disrespecting -women/2195491001/.

Jennifer Shepard Payne, PhD, LCSW, is founder and owner of DTG Counseling and Consulting, a private practice where she provides acceptance and commitment therapy (ACT) counseling and coaching primarily to African Americans of faith suffering from anxiety or trauma. For several years, Payne has been working on culturally tailoring ACT for African American communities, both clinically and via research. She is research faculty with the Kennedy Krieger Center for Child and Family Traumatic Stress, and assistant professor in the department of psychiatry at Johns Hopkins University School of Medicine. For more information, visit her website at: www.poof-pullingoutoffire.com. She lives in Baltimore, MD.

Afterword writer **Robyn D. Walser, PhD,** is director of TL Consultation and Psychological Services, and codirector of Bay Area Trauma Recovery Clinical Services. As a licensed clinical psychologist, she maintains an international training, consulting, and therapy practice. Walser has authored and coauthored several books, including *The Heart of ACT* and *Learning ACT*.

Real change *is* possible

For more than forty-five years, New Harbinger has published proven-effective self-help books and pioneering workbooks to help readers of all ages and backgrounds improve mental health and well-being, and achieve lasting personal growth. In addition, our spirituality books offer profound guidance for deepening awareness and cultivating healing, self-discovery, and fulfillment.

Founded by psychologist Matthew McKay and Patrick Fanning, New Harbinger is proud to be an independent, employee-owned company. Our books reflect our core values of integrity, innovation, commitment, sustainability, compassion, and trust. Written by leaders in the field and recommended by therapists worldwide, New Harbinger books are practical, accessible, and provide real tools for real change.

newharbingerpublications

MORE BOOKS from
NEW HARBINGER PUBLICATIONS

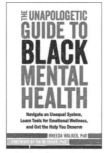
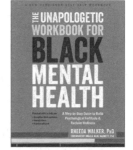

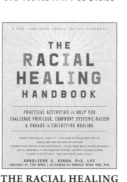

Did you know there are **free tools** you can download for this book?

Free tools are things like **worksheets, guided meditation exercises**, and **more** that will help you get the most out of your book.

You can download free tools for this book—whether you bought or borrowed it, in any format, from any source—from the New Harbinger website. All you need is a NewHarbinger.com account. Just use the URL provided in this book to view the free tools that are available for it. Then, click on the "download" button for the free tool you want, and follow the prompts that appear to log in to your NewHarbinger.com account and download the material.

You can also save the free tools for this book to your **Free Tools Library** so you can access them again anytime, just by logging in to your account! Just look for this button on the book's free tools page.

+ Save this to my free tools library

If you need help accessing or downloading free tools, visit **newharbinger.com/faq** or contact us at **customerservice@newharbinger.com**.